Strength and
Weight Training
for Young Athletes

Strength and Weight Training for Young Athletes

SCOTT ROBERTS and BEN WEIDER

CONTEMPORARY
BOOKS

CHICAGO

Library of Congress Cataloging-in-Publication Data

Roberts, Scott.
    Strength and weight training for young athletes / Scott Roberts
and Ben Weider ; foreword by Paul DeMayo.
       p.   cm.
    Includes bibliographical references and index.
    ISBN 0-8092-3697-4 (paper)
    1. Weight training.   2. Bodybuilding.   I. Weider, Ben, 1923–
II. Title.
GV546.R59   1994
613.7′1—dc20   94-14017
                                              CIP

Photos by Pam Brown, Tay Robertson, and Candice DeLazzer

Published by Contemporary Books, Inc.
Two Prudential Plaza, Chicago, Illinois 60601-6790
Manufactured in the United States of America
International Standard Book Number: 0-8092-3697-4
10   9   8   7   6   5   4   3   2   1

This book is dedicated to my father, William Owen Roberts. My father is

- one of the most knowledgeable weight training experts I have ever met
- a good friend who has always been there when I needed him the most
- a great "papa" to my sons
- the one person who has motivated me the most to aspire to be the very best that I can be

Thanks for all you have done for me, Dad. I love you!

—S.O.R.

Contents

Foreword

I first started lifting weights seriously when I was 18 years old. I enjoyed working out so much, I eventually got into serious bodybuilding. I had developed so much by the time I was 20 that people really started to keep an eye on me. My training became more serious and occupied more and more of my time. In 1991 I entered the National Physique Committee (NPC) Junior National Bodybuilding Championship. To everyone's surprise (except mine), I won it! In 1992 and 1993 I placed in the top three of the National Bodybuilding Championships.

Throughout the bodybuilding world, I am known as "Quadzilla" for my exceptionally well-defined quadriceps. I have appeared in *Flex* magazine, *Muscle & Fitness* magazine, *Ironman*, *Muscle Magazine International*, and *Muscle Media 2000*. Strength and weight training has helped me to become an excellent athlete, a highly recognized and respected bodybuilder, and a better overall person.

Strength and weight training can help you as well. A stronger athlete is a better athlete. People often ask me what advice I would give young, aspiring bodybuilders and athletes. My advice is really quite simple.

- Check with your doctor before starting a serious weight training program.
- Use an adult spotter when lifting weights.
- Never fool around in the weight room.
- Always use good equipment, such as Weider Sporting Goods.
- Make sure to warm up and cool down.
- *Never* use drugs . . . period!
- Always use good form.
- Never show off or try to outperform someone else in the weight room.

- Never lift more weight than you are capable of lifting safely.
- Balance your workout routine with other priorities, such as school and family.
- Don't let your workouts become the most important thing in your life.
- Set realistic goals for yourself, and keep making new ones.
- Above all, have fun!

I wish I'd had a copy of *Strength and Weight Training for Young Athletes* when I was starting out. Scott Roberts and Ben Weider have written a comprehensive, straightforward book, full of practical and useful information. This book contains all a young athlete needs to know to get started on a strength and weight training program.

Follow my advice, and the advice offered in this book, and you will gain strength. I wish you all the best and challenge you to become the best you can be!

See you in the gym.

Paul DeMayo
1991 NPC Junior National Champion

Preface

Strength is important for everyone! Having good strength helps people live healthier and longer lives. Recent studies have shown that 8- and 9-year-olds as well as 80- and 90-year-olds can gain significant levels of strength through resistance training. Athletes can perform better, police officers and firefighters can do their jobs better, older people can get around better, and kids can do better in sports by having good strength. Adequate strength helps you to avoid injuries, excel in sports, have more energy, and simply feel better. Strength training has truly become a lifetime pursuit and "fitness phenomenon." Today you can go into any gym and see children, moms and dads, and even grandparents lifting weights.

This book provides essential information on developing strength in young athletes. Because strength is such an important part of health- and performance-related fitness, both adults and young adults need to participate in some form of regular strength training. It was once thought that children and adolescents should not participate in strength training programs because of the risk of injuries to their developing musculoskeletal systems. But now there is a growing body of research that has given rise to guidelines from medical and sports science organizations that justify and encourage strength training for children and adolescents. Such prestigious organizations as the National Strength and Conditioning Association, the American Orthopaedic Society for Sports Medicine, and the American Physical Therapy Association support supervised resistance training for young people.

Strength and Weight Training for Young Athletes is a valuable reference for coaches, parents, young athletes, and physical educators. This book emphasizes a variety of strength and resistance training methods, besides weights. You don't need a weight training gym or expensive equipment to get stronger. The purpose of this book is to help young athletes learn how to develop strength safely and effectively, through a variety of methods.

We hope that this book will help athletes of all abilities develop a better understanding of strength and resistance training principles and instill a desire to learn more about exercise, fitness, and strength training. It doesn't matter if your goal is to become an Olympic or professional athlete, to do better in high school sports, or just to look and feel better. *Strength and Weight Training for Young Athletes* will help you. We wish you the very best in your athletic and life endeavors. Good luck!

Scott O. Roberts, Ph.D., C.S.C.S.
Ben Weider, C.M., Ph.D.

A Word About the International Federation of Bodybuilders

The International Federation of Bodybuilders (IFBB) was founded in 1946 by Ben and Joe Weider. The IFBB has affiliates in 156 countries, including the People's Republic of China. It is recognized by more than 90 national Olympic committees and government sport agencies that control amateur sport in their countries. As the premier organization that coordinates and regulates the sport of bodybuilding throughout the world, the IFBB is supported by millions of youngsters around the world who want to keep healthy and fit through exercise. The IFBB promotes fitness and a healthy lifestyle; discourages the use of tobacco, alcohol, and drugs; and follows the International Olympic Committee guidelines for drug control.

Strength and Weight Training for Young Athletes is based on the founding principles of the IFBB. The authors of this book encourage and challenge you to follow the principles listed in the IFBB creed. When you do, you will be part of a team of thousands of athletes and bodybuilders who have found success in athletics and in life through regular exercise and healthy living. Remember always to try to do the best you can; that is all anyone, including yourself, can ever ask of you. Winners in life are made, not born. So go out and make yourself a winner.

For more information on the International Federation of Bodybuilders, write to:
IFBB
2875 Bates Road
Montreal, Quebec, Canada H3S 1B7

THE INTERNATIONAL FEDERATION OF BODYBUILDERS CREED

WE BELIEVE in total physical fitness—mental as well as physical—and are convinced that the best citizens are produced by educating the whole man.

WE BELIEVE that total physical fitness can best be obtained through good health habits, adequate nutrition and planned systematic physical exercise.

WE BELIEVE that sports and games of all kinds can contribute greatly to the total fitness of those who participate. Especially important is the vigorous training which precedes successful participation.

WE BELIEVE in the use of modern, scientific methods of training to produce the best possible results in the shortest possible time.

WE BELIEVE in total fitness for all, but are convinced that properly supervised competitive athletic activities have an important place in our society.

WE BELIEVE that our athletes should be given every opportunity to develop their potential to the limit, not only for personal satisfaction and national prestige, but also to serve as stirring examples to others.

WE BELIEVE that with increasing automation the need for exercise becomes steadily greater and the role of the coach and physical educator even more important.

WE BELIEVE that progressive resistance exercise involving gradually increasing work-loads is absolutely essential for the development of muscular strength.

WE BELIEVE that muscular endurance can only be developed through vigorous sustained effort over increasing periods of time.

WE BELIEVE that a vigorous strength-building and endurance-building program is necessary to increase the efficiency of the cardio-vascular system and hence improve over-all physical fitness.

WE BELIEVE that only through regular, planned, purposeful practice is it possible to develop a high degree of neuro-muscular skill.

WE BELIEVE in the development of a well-muscled, symmetrical physique along with all of the attributes mentioned above, not only to achieve success on the athletic field but also to enable the individual to meet the varying demands of everyday life.

"Bodybuilding is important for nation building."
Ben Weider, C.M., Ph.D.,
International President of the IFBB

Reprinted by permission of Ben Weider.

Acknowledgments

Many people helped us write this book. We would like to acknowledge and thank the following individuals. Without them, this book would not have been possible.

- Joe Weider (the Trainer of Champions), for helping to instill the importance of muscular development and exercise to millions of people
- Tom Deters, Associate Publisher and Editor-in-Chief of the premier magazine on strength training and bodybuilding: *Muscle & Fitness* magazine
- Dr. Rich Fields, for contributing the exercise instructions and selecting the sport-specific exercises in Chapter 11
- Taylor, John, Kathleen, Reece, Thomas, Michael, Stephen, Brett, Peter, LeRon, Christy, Nathan, Charles, Robyn, Dyral, Dana, Joe, Jennifer, Matthew, Eric, David, and Jose, for being such great models
- Eric Weider and the entire staff at Weider Sporting Goods, for supplying much of the exercise equipment seen in the photos
- The editors at *Flex* magazine
- Dennis Kirkley, for assisting with the selection of the exercises
- Andy and the gang at Defined Fitness, for letting us use their gym
- The University of New Mexico, for letting us use their gym
- Pam Brown, for her photography expertise
- Wayne Westcott, Ph.D., and Rich Fields, Ph.D., for their thoughtful comments and suggestions about the first draft
- Nancy Crossman, Georgene Sainati, Kristen Carr, Cyndy Raucci, Kathy Willhoite, Dana Draxten, Jan Geist, and the entire staff at Contemporary Books
- My wife, Julia, for her love, support, and understanding throughout this project
- Steve Block and his staff at Spri, Inc.
- Bob Davis and Strength of America in Mesa, AZ
- Paul DeMayo, for writing the Foreword

Part I
Training Fundamentals

1   Developing Muscular Strength and Endurance in Young Athletes

Muscular strength is an important component of physical fitness for both boys and girls. Strength is required to perform basic motor skills such as running, jumping, and throwing. Good strength also helps prevent injuries, improve sports performance, and improve overall health. Within the last 10 to 15 years, a great deal has been learned about the safety and effectiveness of strength and weight training for young athletes. This chapter focuses on some of the most important information and facts.

DEFINING YOUNG ATHLETES

Throughout this book the term *young athletes* is used frequently. Young athletes are those athletes who are not yet adults (18 years or older). This book specifically addresses young athletes between the ages of 13 and 18. By the age of 13, most children are physically and emotionally mature enough to participate in a structured

strength and weight training program, like those outlined in this book. Although it is important for children of all ages to be involved in activities that develop strength, there is not enough room in this book to address all of the special needs and guidelines for younger children. To obtain an excellent book on developing strength in children, the authors suggest you get a copy of *Developing Strength in Children: A Comprehensive Approach* by Scott Roberts, by writing to the National Association of Sport and Physical Education, 1900 Association Drive, Reston, VA 22091.

Three other terms are frequently used throughout this book: *prepubescent, pubescent,* and *adolescent.* Each of these terms refers to a different period of human growth and development. The prepubescent period is the period before children develop secondary sex characteristics (breasts, pubic hair, etc.). This period is sometimes referred to as middle childhood and includes females ages 7 to 10 and males ages 7 to 12. The pubescent period is signaled by the appearance of secondary sex characteristics (the development of genitals, including the appearance of pubic hair). Puberty generally occurs between 11 and 13 years in girls and 13 and 15 in boys. The adolescent period is a time of rapid growth and development, often referred to as the adolescent growth spurt period. The adolescent period signals sexual maturity. Adolescence generally starts around 14 to 18 years in females and 16 to 18 years in males. Regular exercise, including some form of resistance training, is important to children of all ages. However, certain activities, such as lifting free weights, are more appropriate for older, adolescent children.

STRENGTH LEVELS OF AMERICAN CHILDREN AND ADOLESCENTS

No matter what research you look at, no matter how you interpret the results, the fact is American children and adolescents do not have good upper-body strength. The results of several large-scale youth fitness tests, such as the President's Council on Physical Fitness Test, have reported that upper-body strength among American children and adolescents is poor. Some of the more alarming statistics include these:

- Part I of the National Children and Youth Fitness Study reported that more than 30 percent of 10- to 11-year-old boys and 60 percent of 10- to 18-year-old girls were unable to perform one chin-up.
- A 1985 study conducted by the President's Council on Physical Fitness and Sports tested 18,857 American schoolchildren ages 6 through 17. The results of the strength tests showed that

40 percent of the boys ages 6 to 12 could not do more than one pull-up and 25 percent could not do any, 70 percent of all girls tested could not do more than one pull-up and 55 percent could not do any, and 45 percent of the boys 6 to 14 and 55 percent of all the girls tested could not hold their chin over a raised bar for more than 10 seconds.

- A 1981–82 test conducted by the Amateur Athletic Union found that 60 percent of the girls tested from ages 6 to 17 could not perform one pull-up. The mean number of pull-ups for boys did not exceed 10 for any age group, 6 to 17.

These results stress the need for regular strength and weight training for children and adolescents. Because many schools today do not have the resources to offer physical education programs, many children get their physical training outside of the school at a YMCA, health club, local recreation center, or home.

THE BENEFITS OF STRENGTH TRAINING FOR YOUNG ATHLETES

The benefits of resistance training for adults have been well established. It has only been within the last 10 to 15 years that much of the research regarding the benefits of strength and resistance training for children and adolescents have been reported.

Injury Prevention
A report by the American Physical Therapy Association concluded that poor physical conditioning of young athletes may be the leading cause of injury in youth sports. A properly designed resistance training program will develop and prepare the muscles

for sport and competition. Although the data to support the contention that resistance training prevents injuries in young athletes is limited, the circumstantial evidence is overwhelming.

All sports place demands on the musculoskeletal system. Although different sports place different demands on the musculoskeletal system, there is general agreement among medical and sports medicine experts that increasing the strength of the adult athlete will enhance performance and decrease the chance of injury. Because it has been demonstrated that children and adolescents can increase strength following resistance training, encouraging them to participate in resistance training to reduce potential injuries is justified.

Improved Sports Performance

Resistance training is an integral part of the preseason training for amateur and professional athletes. It helps prepare the athlete both mentally and physically for the upcoming season. Several studies have shown that certain sports performances in young athletes, such as jumping ability, speed, and strength, can be improved by following a structured resistance training program.

Improved Health

A resistance training program can provide numerous health benefits. In addition to improvements in muscular strength and endurance, studies have demonstrated that young athletes can achieve the following benefits from resistance training: improved flexibility (less risk of injury, better performance in sports), favorable improvements in body composition (low percentage of body fat and greater percentages of lean body mass), reductions in blood lipids (lower risk of developing heart disease), improved cardiorespiratory function (better endurance), and decreased blood pressure (lower risk of developing heart disease).

SUMMARY OF THE BENEFITS OF STRENGTH TRAINING FOR YOUNG ATHLETES

1. Prevention of cardiovascular disease
2. Reduction and control of high blood pressure and childhood obesity
3. Improvement in the ability to perform basic motor skills
4. Possible prevention of injuries
5. Improved self-confidence and self-image
6. Early development of good posture
7. Greater ease and efficiency in performing motor tasks and sport skills
8. Better performance on nationwide fitness tests
9. Early development of coordination and balance
10. The establishment of fitness as a lifetime interest
11. Improved flexibility
12. Favorable improvements in body composition

CONTROVERSIES IN YOUTH STRENGTH TRAINING

For the majority of the twentieth century, the idea of children and even adolescents participating in strength and resistance training programs gained little support from physicians and physical educators, despite the evidence of poor strength levels in children. Much of the evidence in supporting the ban on prepubescent resistance training evolved from several early scientific reports that concluded that young children were not able to gain strength before puberty and that they were more susceptible to injuries because of their developing

WHAT IS THE GROWTH PLATE?

The term *growth plate* is often mentioned when discussing youth sports and strength and weight training for young athletes. The growth plate is the area at the ends of the long bones (femur, tibia, radius, etc.) which allows longitudinal growth to occur. Thus, the main shafts of the bones are hard, but the growth plates have not yet fused and are the site of growth. The growth plate consists of cartilage but is eventually replaced by bone, at which time (near the end of the adolescent period) growth ends. Growth plate injuries do occur in children and adolescents. Some of the more common causes of growth plate injuries are everyday accidents and participation in sports such as baseball, skiing, football, gymnastics, and long-distance running. There is, however, little if any evidence to support the belief that properly supervised resistance training causes harm to the growth plate or musculoskeletal system in young athletes.

musculoskeletal systems. Fortunately, new information regarding the safety, effectiveness, and health benefits of resistance training for children is now likely to reverse past skepticism.

Myth #1
Children are not able to develop strength beyond that normally associated with normal growth and development.

Myth: One of the first scientific studies to investigate the effects of resistance training on strength in prepubescent and pubescent boys was conducted back in the early 1970s. A group of prepubescent and a group of adolescent subjects performed a circuit of eight weight training exercises three times a week for eight weeks. After eight weeks, the kids were re-tested and only the adolescent group had gained strength. This difference in strength levels led to the false conclusion that prepubescent children cannot gain significant strength until maturity is reached because of the lack of male hormones (i.e., testosterone).

Fact: Prepubescent children are able to make significant strength gains following supervised resistance training, regardless of the amount of testosterone present. As with women and older individuals (who don't have a great deal of testosterone), strength gains are the result of better coordination of muscle fibers and muscle groups. More than 20 scientific studies performed since the early studies of the '70s have demonstrated significant strength gains in prepubescent children and adolescents following resistance training.

Myth #2
Children should not lift weights or participate in resistance training programs because of the risk of injury to the growth plates.

Myth: Several early medical reports recommended that children not participate in weight training because the developing bones and musculature of young children are more susceptible to injuries than those of adults. In addition, several studies have reported growth plate injuries in adolescent children who participated in strength training exercises. These and other reports have recommended that children avoid any formal strength training programs until reaching puberty, at which time the growth plates have fused and the long bones are less susceptible to injuries.

Fact: Several recent research studies have looked at the safety of resistance training in prepubescent children. In two of the studies, safety was monitored via physician evaluation before, during, and after training, and by a sophisticated x-ray technique called musculoskeletal scintigraph. Both of these studies found no evidence of damage to the epiphyses, bone, or muscle following supervised resistance training. Growth plate injuries have occurred in adolescents during resistance training, although they are rare. The type of injury most commonly reported has been injury to the wrist that occurred during excessive overhead lifts, which are not recommended for young children.

Myth #3
There is not enough evidence to support a structured resistance training program for children.

Myth: Many have argued that there is not enough evidence to support resistance training before puberty; and even if there were, they question what the benefits would be. Thus, young athletes should not participate in any formal strength and resistance training until more scientific evidence is available to support it.

Fact: Within the last 20 years, several important scientific studies have demonstrated that prepubescent children are able to make significant strength gains following supervised resistance training, and furthermore, that such training is very safe. It is important to point out that, although there has been a great deal of literature published recently regarding the safety and effectiveness of structured,

supervised resistance training programs for young athletes, further research is needed to examine the long-term effects of such training and the impact resistance training has on injury prevention and athletic performance. However, the majority of the evidence to date points to the conclusion that prepubescent and adolescent resistance training is safe, that it is effective in developing muscular strength and endurance, and that numerous benefits are possible following such training. In fact, so much evidence exists that experts are unwilling to set a definite age limit below which strength training should never be done.

PROFESSIONAL GUIDELINES AND RECOMMENDATIONS

Three professional organizations have published position stands on prepubescent strength training: the American Academy of Pediatrics (AAP), the National Strength and Conditioning Association (NSCA), and the American Orthopaedic Society for Sports Medicine (AOSSM).

In 1983, the American Academy of Pediatrics developed an information guide for pediatricians regarding weight training for children (American Academy of Pediatrics on Sports Medicine 1983). Although the AAP's position paper reported the benefits of weight training for athletes, the general theme of the paper discouraged strength training for prepubertal children for the following reasons:

- Prepubertal boys do not significantly increase muscle mass from weight training because of insufficient male hormones.
- Minimal benefits are obtained from weight training in the prepubertal athlete.

- Weight lifting is a competitive sport with a high injury rate that should not be practiced by prepubescent children.

The AAP went on to state, however, that "weight training, because of the benefits and lower potential for injury, is a reasonably safe technique that, when supervised, can be endorsed for youths."

In 1990, the AAP released an updated version of their earlier report (American Academy of Pediatrics on Sports Medicine 1990). In this report, the AAP recommended the following:

- Strength training programs for prepubescent, pubescent, and postpubescent athletes should be permitted only if conducted by well-trained adults. The adults should be qualified to plan programs appropriate to the athlete's stage of maturation, which should be assessed by medical personnel.

Because of the concern over injury and the increased interest in strength training for youths, the National Strength and Conditioning Association developed a position stand on prepubescent strength training in 1985. The NSCA believes that, when performed properly, strength training programs for the prepubescent athlete can improve strength, self-image, and motor performance, and can reduce injury.

In August 1985, eight sports medicine groups attended the American Orthopaedic Society for Sports Medicine's workshop on strength training. The major organizations present at that workshop included AOSSM, AAP, NSCA, American College of Sports Medicine, National Athletic Trainers Association, President's Council on Physical Fitness and Sports, U.S. Olympic Committee, and the Society of Pediatric Orthopaedics.

The consensus of these groups was that strength training for prepubescent boys and girls is safe with proper program design, instruction, and supervision. In addition, the overall groups' position was that the benefits of prepubescent strength training do outweigh the risks.

FACTORS INFLUENCING STRENGTH DEVELOPMENT IN YOUNG ATHLETES

Age
Strength gains are highly correlated to age. As children approach puberty, the ability to develop strength reaches a peak.

Lean Body Mass
Both aerobic capacity and strength are highly correlated to lean body mass. Regular training results in a decrease in fatness and an increase in fat free mass, or lean body mass. Children involved in regular physical activity generally display greater percentages of lean body mass and lower percentages of fat.

Sex
Before adolescence, the strength of boys and girls shows little difference. Once sexual maturity is reached, males generally perform better on most tests of strength than do girls. The greater strength of boys is primarily related to the presence of the male hormone testosterone.

Hormones
Up to the age of puberty in the male, the level of testosterone is too low to promote muscle hypertrophy. The trainability of children increases rapidly during puberty as the level of testosterone increases. Strength increases rapidly during this pe-

riod in the male, compared to the female, even without training.

SIGNIFICANCE OF THE ADOLESCENT GROWTH SPURT PERIOD

Strength and agility generally improve dramatically during middle childhood and adolescence. The adolescent growth spurt in males is magnified, primarily due to the increase in male hormones. Adolescent athletes are often able to make remarkable increases in strength gains during this period. If an athlete has a solid foundation of training from which to build, during adolescence he or she can start training more frequently, more intensely, and for a longer duration. One caution: do not overtrain. Young adolescent athletes need to be cautioned about overtraining because of the possibility of injury to the growth plates. During adolescence, the growth plates are getting ready to permanently fuse together. At this point, the growth plates are thicker and more porous, which makes them more susceptible to injury. In addition, the growth spurt may increase the susceptibility to growth plate injury because of an increase in muscle-tendon tightness about the joints, which results in a loss of flexibility.

STRENGTH AND WEIGHT TRAINING FOR GIRLS

Girls and young women should be encouraged to get involved in a strength and weight training program. Just like boys, girls can gain significant levels of strength from training. The benefits of this training are the same for both sexes. Today, women of all ages are participating in strength and weight training with terrific results.

Women are often concerned that they will get "really big" muscles from strength training. Actually, it is physiologically impossible for women to develop huge muscles like those seen on male bodybuilders. Yes, it is true that muscles will be slightly larger and more defined after strength training, but a woman's femininity will not be lost in any way as a result. Strength training is simply a great way for young women to get in shape!

KEY POINTS

- Muscular strength and endurance is an important component of physical fitness for both boys and girls.
- This book specifically addresses young athletes between the ages of 13 and 18. By the age of 13, most children are physically and emotionally mature enough to participate in a structured strength and weight training program.
- American children and adolescents do not have good upper-body strength, as demonstrated in several large-scale youth fitness tests.
- Poor physical conditioning of young athletes may be the leading cause of injury in youth sports.
- In addition to improvements in muscular strength and endurance, studies have demonstrated that young athletes can achieve numerous health benefits from resistance training.
- Prepubescent children are able to make significant strength gains following supervised resistance training, regardless of the amount of testosterone present.
- Growth plate injuries have occurred in adolescents during resistance training, although they are rare. The

type of injury most commonly reported has been injury to the wrist that occurred during excessive overhead lifts, which are not recommended for young children.

- Before adolescence, the strength of boys and girls shows little difference. Once sexual maturity is reached, males generally perform better on most tests of strength than do girls. This is primarily related to the presence of the male hormone testosterone.

- Just like boys, girls can gain significant levels of strength from training.

Principles of
2   Strength and Weight Training

The history of strength training probably dates back to the beginning of the Olympic Games. It has been said that the great Olympic champion Milo of Crotono, who lived in Greece in the sixth century B.C., used to carry around a baby bull on his shoulders to improve his strength. As the bull grew heavier with age, Milo improved his strength. Since then, strength training has developed into a high-tech, billion dollar business. Strength training has become a popular way to improve athletic ability, look and feel better, relieve stress, and improve health. This chapter presents some of the fundamental principles of strength and weight training.

DEFINING MUSCULAR STRENGTH AND ENDURANCE

Muscular strength is defined as the greatest amount of force a muscle, or group of muscles, can produce during one maximal contraction, whereas *muscular endurance* is the ability of a muscle, or muscle group, to perform repeated contractions for an extended period of time. Although they have different definitions, muscular strength and muscular endurance are very similar. If you do not have good muscular strength, you probably won't have good muscular endurance, and vice versa.

> Muscular strength and endurance are vital to our health and well-being and to our ability to perform in athletics and at work.

Adequate muscular strength and endurance are vital to each of us when we lift, push, and pull objects. A high degree of muscular strength allows a tackle to push his opponent out of the way, a powerlifter to lift the weight up and over his head, and a pole-vaulter to pull himself up and over the bar. Muscular strength and endurance are also important to our ability to perform routine chores, like taking out the garbage. Firefighters, police officers, and garbage collectors all need good strength to perform well at their jobs.

Types of Muscular Contractions

The two basic types of muscular contractions are isotonic and isometric. An *isotonic* contraction (iso meaning equal and tonic meaning tension) is a type of contraction in which the muscles generate varying force against a constant resistance (e.g., free-weight lifting). During an isotonic movement, the force or tension required to lift a weight through a given range of motion will vary according to where it is in the range of the movement. For example, when performing a biceps curl with a 50-pound dumbbell, the tension or force (F) is 50

Isotonic exercise: biceps curl—zero degrees

pounds at the start of the movement (zero degrees). Force is greatest at 90 degrees (F = 65 pounds) and lowest at 180 degrees (F = 32.5 pounds). The point of the greatest resistance is often referred to as the *sticking point*.

Isotonic movements consist of both *concentric* and *eccentric* muscle contractions.

The concentric phase of an isotonic muscular contraction occurs when the muscles contract and the muscle fibers shorten (e.g., lifting the weight up during a biceps curl). The eccentric phase of an isotonic contraction occurs when the muscles relax and the muscle fibers lengthen (e.g., releasing the weight down during a biceps curl).

Isotonic exercise: biceps curl—90 degrees

Isotonic exercise: biceps curl—180 degrees

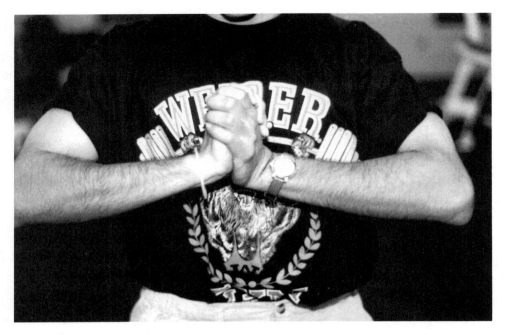

Isometric exercise

An *isometric* contraction is a static contraction in which the muscles generate force against an immovable object with no muscle shortening taking place. Attempting to lift or push an immovable object (a car with its brakes on) is an example of an isometric contraction.

DEFINING RESISTANCE AND STRENGTH TRAINING

Resistance Training

Resistance training is any method used to develop strength through lifting, pulling, or pushing. Children and adolescents should be encouraged to participate in regular exercise that involves repetitive movements against an opposing force. It is important to note that children and adolescents can develop strength through a variety of activities including participation in sports, weight training, manual resistance exercises, and simple play.

Strength Training

Strength can be defined as the ability to exert muscular force against resistance. Strength training is defined as the use of different progressive resistance exercise methods designed to increase one's ability to exert muscular force against resistance. The desired effect is a measurable increase in strength. Strength training is part of a comprehensive fitness program also involving flexibility and aerobics.

Weight Versus Resistance Training

Weight training typically uses common equipment such as free weights or machines to provide the resistance needed to increase strength. As adaptation occurs, more weight is added to provide additional resistance.

Resistance training includes the use of multiple forms of resistance when performing different exercises. Resistance can be provided by opposing muscle groups, the individual's body weight, elastic bands or tubing, and with free weights or machines. The intended outcome of resistance training is increased muscular strength and endurance. Instead of adding on more weight to change the resistance as adaptation occurs, the intensity of the exercise and/or duration of exercise is increased.

Because resistance training is more comprehensive in scope, and because weight training assumes that free weights or weight machines are needed, the terms *resistance* or *strength* training should be stressed over weight training when applied to young athletes. Because free weights or weight machines are not always available, this book describes the use of multiple forms of resistance training. Resistance training can be taught to young athletes so they will benefit from it without the need for expensive equipment.

STRENGTH AND WEIGHT TRAINING FUNDAMENTALS

Overload
Gains in strength result from repeatedly overloading the muscle through a combination of increases in intensity and duration. Training programs need to be monitored and adjusted with time so that muscles are stressed and forced to adapt. If you lift 100 pounds every workout for one month, you will maintain your level of strength, but you will not improve it.

Load
Load is the intensity of exercise, and in resistance training it refers to the amount of resistance or weight used. Before any weight/resistance is utilized, proper technique should be demonstrated and practiced for each exercise. The next step is to

gradually apply weight/resistance until 10 to 15 repetitions can be performed in a set.

Repetition
Repetition refers to the number of times an exercise is performed per exercise session or set. Young athletes should perform 8 to 12 repetitions for upper-body exercises and 15 to 20 repetitions for lower-body exercises. Once the predetermined maximum number of repetitions per set is achieved, the weight or the maximum number of repetitions should be increased.

Sets
One to three sets of each exercise should be performed, utilizing approximately 8 to 10 different exercises. In the early stages of training, one set of each exercise should be performed until the athlete has demonstrated proper form and is acclimated to resistance training.

Rest
Rest is the amount of time between sets. Young athletes should be encouraged to rest for one to two minutes between exercises. Children, especially, often do not perceive stress as an adult might. Therefore, it is important to make sure children and adolescents get adequate rest between exercises, as well as between exercise sessions.

Frequency
Frequency refers to the number of training sessions in a given amount of time. Two to three exercise sessions per week is recommended, followed by at least one day of rest between workouts. As young athletes mature, they will naturally become involved in a variety of activities, including after-school sports. Resistance training sessions should be modified to incorporate changes in children's activity patterns.

Progression

Many young athletes try to lift too much weight early on in their training program. Such practices often lead to injuries and chronic fatigue. To maintain maximal stimulus, the resistance and/or number of repetitions must be increased periodically. Once an athlete is able to lift the preestablished number of repetitions, a small (5 to 10 percent) increase in resistance can be made. When there is an increase in the weight being lifted, there should be a reduction in the repetitions (i.e., if the preestablished number of repetitions was 12, after an increase in weight, a new repetition maximum might be seven or eight). As the athlete adjusts to the new training stimulus, he or she will soon be able to lift the new weight 12 times, at which point a new weight and repetition maximum will be established.

PROGRESSION FORMULA	
(Preestablished repetitions = 12–15)	
REPETITIONS COMPLETED	ADJUSTMENT (IN POUNDS)
<7	−15
8–9	−10
10–11	−5
12–15	0
16–17	+5
18–19	+10
>20	+15

Note. From *Weight Training: Steps to Success* (p. 69) by T. R. Baechle and B. R. Groves, Champaign, IL: Leisure Press. Copyright 1992 by Leisure Press. Reprinted by permission.

Specificity of Training

Training programs should be designed with specific goals and objectives in mind. The exercises chosen should reflect the desired outcome. For the majority of young athletes, specificity of training is not as important as it will be in later years. Children and adolescents should participate in a variety of activities to develop a wide range of skills.

Reversibility

When muscles are overloaded, they adapt by getting stronger and larger. When the exercise stimulus is removed, the training adaptations reverse. If children do not remain active (e.g., over summer break or a holiday), they may notice some changes in their strength levels.

Warm-Up Period

Warm-up exercises increase the temperature of the muscle and increase its elasticity, both of which improve the muscle's ability to perform work, as well as reduce the risk of muscle and joint injury. Warm-up activities should consist of some stretching and large muscle activities, such as walking or jogging.

Cool-Down Period

The purpose of cooling down is to lower the muscle temperature and metabolic rate. Cool-down activities can be similar to warm-up activities. Watch athletes closely during the cool-down session for signs of overtraining.

HOW MUSCLES GET STRONGER AND BIGGER

Hypertrophy

Hypertrophy describes the increase in muscle size following resistance training. Hypertrophy typically does not occur in prepubescent children. As children reach maturity, their ability to increase muscle size improves dramatically.

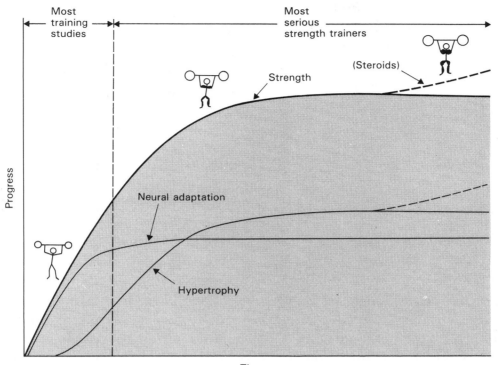

How Muscles Get Stronger and Bigger

Neural Adaptations

Neural (nervous system) adaptation is the primary mechanism responsible for improvements in strength. When a muscle is stimulated to contract, one or many motor units may be stimulated. A motor unit is a nerve connected to one or more muscle fibers. The greater the number of motor units stimulated, the greater the strength of contraction, the more weight can be lifted. When motor units are recruited in selected patterns, individuals are able to lift more

weight. Strength training improves the nervous system's ability to coordinate the recruitment of muscle fibers.

ADVANCED TRAINING TECHNIQUES

Eccentric Loading

Remember that an eccentric contraction occurs when the muscle contracts and the muscle fibers lengthen. Eccentric loading, or performing "negatives," allows you to develop strength while maintaining control of the weight. An example of performing a negative is to have someone hand you a weight in the contracted position and then slowly release the weight to the start of the exercise movement. Negatives are a popular and effective technique to develop strength and overcome sticking points, but they also seem to cause more fatigue and soreness than other methods.

Plyometric Training
Plyometric training is a technique used to develop explosive strength and power. A plyometric exercise consists of a quick ec-

---

Under no circumstances should young athletes be allowed to perform plyometric exercise without direct supervision by a knowledgeable coach.

---

centric stretch followed by a powerful concentric contraction. The sudden stretch causes certain receptors in the muscles to stimulate a more powerful contraction. An example of a plyometric exercise is jumping off a bench, bending at the knees, and jumping back up onto the bench. Plyometric training is an effective method of improving muscular strength and endurance as well as power and speed, but it can cause injuries if not performed correctly.

Circuit Training
Circuit training is a form of strength training that consists of a series of strength and aerobic exercises. It is an effective way of developing strength and flexibility but has little effect on aerobic endurance.

Example of a Circuit Workout
Station 1—Hamstring and calf stretch
Station 2—Push-ups (30 repetitions)
Station 3—Rope skipping (100 repetitions)
Station 4—Bench press (12 repetitions at 75 percent effort)

Station 5—Triceps extensions (8 to 12 repetitions with each arm)

UNSAFE WEIGHT TRAINING METHODS FOR YOUNG ATHLETES

Power Lifting
Power lifting, or lifting in a competitive setting to determine the maximum amount of weight an individual can lift, is not recommended for young athletes. This type of lifting is discouraged because of a higher risk of injuries associated with it. Young athletes should not lift maximal amounts until age 14 to 16. In addition, the primary focus of resistance training should, at least initially, be on developing proper technique, learning the exercises, and developing an interest for lifting.

Power lifting, one-repetition maximum lifting, and competitive lifting should be discouraged for young children.

One-Repetition Maximum
The one-repetition maximum (1RM) method is used to establish starting weights for different exercises. It involves an individual lifting the maximum amount of weight he or she can lift for a particular exercise. Once an individual's 1RM is established, different percentages of the 1RM weight are used when performing selected exercises. Young athletes should not perform 1RM, power, or competitive lifting. The methods for choosing the correct starting weight for youths are discussed in more detail in Chapter 8.

STRENGTH TRAINING EQUIPMENT

Variable Resistance Equipment

Remember that during an isotonic movement the weight is constant, but the muscular force needed to move the weight is not. The disadvantage of isotonic testing and training equipment is that the resistance is always changing throughout the range of motion. In an effort to create a more constant resistance during exercise movements, companies have developed variable or accommodating resistance equipment, such as Nautilus and Universal equipment. Nautilus equipment uses specially shaped devices (kidney-shaped cams) to alter the resistance throughout the range of motion, whereas Universal equipment uses a special design to achieve the same results. By using varying or accommodating equipment, the force needed to move weight is increased at the joint angle and muscle length that is mechanically advantaged (180 degrees during the biceps curl) and decreased at the joint angle that is mechanically disadvantaged (90 degrees during the biceps curl).

Dumbbells

Barbells

Squat rack

Isokinetic Exercise Equipment

An isokinetic movement is one in which the length of the muscle changes while the contraction is performed at a constant velocity. With isokinetic devices, the resistance is constant and maximum throughout the full range of motion. No matter how much force is applied, the speed of the movement is always the same. With isokinetic equipment, peak power or force can be achieved throughout the full range of motion. There are a variety of isokinetic devices available today (Cybex, Biodex, Lido, KinCom).

TRAINING SMART
Avoid Overtraining

Overtraining occurs when performance in athletics or training plateaus or decreases over time. Usually overtraining is caused by poor program design, lack of adequate rest, and by not keeping a training log. Athletes and coaches should plan training sessions so the intensity of the workouts increases gradually over time and the athlete has adequate time to rest. Athletes need to report any of the following conditions to coaches or parents, because they can be signs of overtraining:

- loss of body weight
- decrease in appetite
- muscle soreness that does not go away, even after rest
- increase in illness, such as colds, flu, etc.
- constipation or diarrhea
- decrease in performance
- lack of desire in training or competing

Causes of Muscle Fatigue and Soreness

Exercising or playing too hard sometimes results in muscle soreness and pain. There are generally two causes of muscle fatigue and soreness: a lack of blood and oxygen supply to the working muscles and actual damage to muscle. Muscle fatigue usually improves with a night's rest, but muscle damage may take 48 to 72 hours or more to get better. Ice is a good treatment for muscle soreness, but if pain lasts for more than 72 hours, a physician should be notified. Muscle soreness can be prevented by taking some precautions:

- stretching before and after a workout
- not lifting more than you are able to
- paying attention to signs of overtraining
- lifting in a slow and controlled manner
- getting plenty of rest

SAFETY CONSIDERATIONS

The risk of injuries to young athletes participating in resistance training programs is very low. However, injuries can occur in any sport or strenuous activity. To minimize the risk of injury during resistance training, these recommendations should be followed:

- A preparticipation physical exam should be performed before an athlete begins any type of conditioning program.
- Competition should always be prohibited.
- Young athletes should be properly supervised at all times.
- Children and adolescents should not be allowed to exercise unless the weight training facility is safe for them.
- Young athletes should never perform single maximal lifts or sudden explosive movements.
- Lifters should not show off and should never lift more weight than they are capable of.
- When lifting a weight up off the floor, the athlete should make sure to keep it close to the body.
- Young athletes should progress gradually, within their limits. Overtraining predisposes the athlete to injuries.
- Young athletes should be taught to breathe properly during exercise movements (exhale during the lifting part of the lift: inhale during the recovery phase).
- A strength and weight training program should be part of a comprehensive fitness program, including aerobic exercise and flexibility training.
- Strength and weight training exercises should be performed throughout the full range of motion.
- Young athletes should never be allowed to use any equipment that is broken or damaged or that they don't fit on properly.

- Young athletes should rest for approximately one to two minutes between each exercise, more if necessary. In addition, children should have scheduled rest days between each training day.
- Young athletes should be encouraged to drink plenty of fluids before, during, and after exercising.
- Athletes should be told that they need to communicate with their coach, parent or teacher when they feel fatigued or when they have been injured.
- All strength and weight training workouts should be preceded by a warm-up period and followed by a cool-down period.
- When using free weights, athletes must always train with a partner.
- If an athlete develops any soreness, fatigue, or pain during a workout, the workout should be modified or canceled.
- Safety goggles, versus prescription glasses, should always be worn during any sporting activity, including strength and weight training.

KEY POINTS

- Young athletes should be encouraged to participate in regular exercise that involves repetitive movements against an opposing force (sports, strength training, etc.).
- Power lifting, or lifting in a competitive setting to determine the maximum amount of weight an individual can lift, is not recommended.
- The primary focus of resistance training should, at least initially, be on developing proper technique, learning the exercises, and developing an interest in lifting.

- Before any exercise is performed, proper technique should be demonstrated for each exercise. The next step is to gradually apply resistance.
- As children develop strength during training, the training stimulus will need to be adjusted. To maintain maximal stimulus, the resistance and/or number of repetitions must be increased.
- A brief warm-up period should precede the exercise session and a brief cool-down should follow the exercise session. Warm-up exercises increase the temperature of the muscle and increase its elasticity, both of which improve the muscle's ability to perform work, as well as reduce the risk of muscle and joint injury. Cool-down activities lower the muscle temperature and metabolic rate.

3 Getting Started

Chapters 1 and 2 presented the fundamentals of strength and weight training. Now it's time to get started. There are a variety of strength and weight training systems. Just pick up any strength training or bodybuilding magazine, and I'll bet you will find a story about a "new" or "revolutionary" technique to improve strength. Unfortunately, many of these new and revolutionary programs have not been scientifically proven to be effective, and thus should be viewed with caution. Virtually all strength and weight training systems are based on a variation of the fundamental principles of strength and weight training (load, repetition, intensity, rest, and frequency). This chapter discusses some of the more common and scientifically proven methods to develop strength.

DETERMINING YOUR GOALS

Before you get started on a strength and weight training program, you need to determine what your individual goals are. Perhaps you want to do better in a particular sport, bulk up to look better, or rehabilitate an injured muscle. Why is it so important to set goals before starting? Because you will achieve faster, safer, and more effective results if you do. Everyone's time is limited these days, even young people's. If you are involved in sports, have homework to do, want to spend time with friends, and also work out, you had better develop a game plan.

Before you go any further, ask yourself the following questions:

1. Why am I interested in starting a strength and weight training program?
2. What are the most important benefits I want to achieve through strength training?
3. How will I fit my workouts into my schedule?

Once you have answered these questions, you are ready to go on.

Steps In Goal Setting

Before you can effectively plan your strength and conditioning program, you need to know what it is you want to accomplish and how you will reach your goals. Here are the steps to take:

1. *State your present situation.*

   Example: I am going to try out for the freshman football team this year, but I don't think I'm big enough or strong enough to make the starting team. I want to improve my chances to play more this year and to prepare for next year.

2. *Write a measurable statement of your goal or objective.*

   Example: I will commit 10 hours a week, for the next five months, to my strength and conditioning program. I will make training a priority in my life.

3. *Identify what you need to do to attain that goal.*

   Example: I will commit six hours a week to my strength training program and four hours to my cardiovascular and skill conditioning.

4. *List the activities necessary for you to carry out your plan of action.*

   Example: (see examples of training programs on pages 150–163).

5. *Decide at which points you are going to review your progress.*

   Example: Each month, I will sit down and review my training log to see how my progress is coming and where I need to make changes in my training program.

EQUIPMENT NEEDS

The specific needs for weight training are discussed in Chapter 8. Otherwise, there are really very few equipment needs. A list of selected exercise equipment can be found in Appendix D. A comfortable shirt should always be worn during a workout to reduce the amount of sweat left behind on a mat or exercise bench. You may want to bring an extra T-shirt or sweatshirt with you to wear after a hard workout. Any type of good quality tennis or cross-training shoe should be worn at all times during a workout to protect against injury and to add stability to the exercise movements. You should also carry a water bottle and towel with you during your workout.

GENERAL TRAINING SYSTEMS

As mentioned earlier, there are probably hundreds of strength and weight training systems. Most of these systems are built on the basic principle of *overload*—a muscle will adapt (increase in strength) when it is stressed to overcome more than it is used to. For the young athlete, it is important to start out with a basic program and modify it with time and training experience.

Periodization System

Periodization, or cycling, is a technique used by virtually all athletes. It allows you to systematically plan your training sessions to avoid overtraining and maximize your workout sessions. With periodization, athletes vary the type, amount, and intensity of training for several weeks, a month, or a whole year. Periodization allows you to perform the same, or similar exercises during each training session, but still vary the workout. This technique allows your body to adapt rapidly, without increased risk of injury.

Start by making a schedule of your workouts for one month. Here is an example of a periodization schedule for one month:

Week One   Low intensity, high volume
           Upper-body exercise—four sets of 10 reps
           Exercise example: Bench press (80 pounds)
           Lower-body exercise—four sets of 15 reps
           Exercise example: Knee extensions (50 pounds)

Week Two   Medium intensity, high volume
           Bench press—four sets of 10 reps (90 pounds)
           Knee extensions—four sets of 15 reps (60 pounds)

Week Three   High intensity, low volume
           Bench press—three sets of 8 reps (100 pounds)
           Knee extensions—three sets of 10 reps (70 pounds)

Week Four   Low intensity, high volume
           Bench press—four sets of 10 reps (80 pounds)
           Knee extensions—four sets of 15 reps (50 pounds)

Pyramid System

The pyramid system has become a popular technique among athletes and bodybuilders. In this system, the athlete performs continuous sets of exercises, progressing from light to heavy resistance, while decreasing the number of repetitions along the way. For example, say an athlete can lift a 25-pound dumbbell 10 times comfortably.

First set—10 reps (25 pounds)
Second set—8 reps (30 pounds)
Third set—6 reps (35 pounds)
Fourth set—8 to 10 reps (20 pounds) (to cool down)

TRAINING PROGRAMS FOR MUSCLE HYPERTROPHY (LARGER MUSCLES)

The objective of strength training is to increase the maximal force and endurance capacity of muscles. One of the adaptations following strength training, besides an increase in strength, is an increase in muscle size. It is possible to gain strength without changes in muscle size. However, for most young athletes and bodybuilders, "bulking up" is one of the best rewards of strength and weight training.

Split Routine System

A split routine system trains different body parts on alternate days in an effort to stimulate hypertrophy of all muscles in a particular area of the body. A typical training routine might be chest, shoulders, and back on Monday, Wednesday, and Friday; and arms, legs, and abdominal muscles on Tuesday, Thursday, and Saturday. Split routines can vary as well. Instead of a six-day training session, you can develop a four-day training session. Split routines allow you to work a particular part of the body one day, and rest that area the next day while you work another body area. Split routine training is not recommended for children because the volume and intensity of training may be too strenuous.

Superset System

With the superset system, opposing muscle groups are worked through exercises performed one right after another. An example of a superset workout would be to perform biceps curls immediately followed by triceps extensions, or leg extensions immediately followed by leg curls. Supersetting is a popular way to increase muscle hypertrophy.

TRAINING FOR GENERAL CONDITIONING

A strength and weight training program for general conditioning should consist of two to three days of strength training, in addition to cardiovascular conditioning (running, swimming, cycling, etc.) for at least 30 to 40 minutes, three days per week. In addition to your strength and cardiovascular conditioning, you might also have to consider your athletic practice schedule. If you are involved in athletics, during the competitive season you will want to reduce the intensity and frequency of your strength training program. It is a good idea to get guidelines from your coach regarding your strength training program before, during, and following an athletic season. Otherwise, if you are involved in a strength and conditioning program for overall physical conditioning and health, try and stay with your program all year long. Remember the principle of *reversibility*: if you stop an exercise program, you will soon lose most of the gains you made from training.

TRAINING FOR SPORT AND PERFORMANCE

A training routine for sport and performance differs from a general conditioning program in that it is more specific. Remember the principle of *specificity*: the body adapts according to the stresses placed on it. Each sport has its own unique physical demands. The soccer player needs a great deal of lower-body strength and endurance, while the tennis player needs a great deal of arm strength and endurance, as well as leg endurance. It is important to focus on the specific muscle groups utilized in a particular sport and develop your training program around exercises that will strengthen those muscle groups. Chapter 11 outlines detailed training programs, using a variety of training techniques for a variety of sports.

REST

The amount of rest between workouts is just as important as the amount of time spent in workouts. Rest is needed between workouts to replace the energy stores in your muscles (glycogen) and to let your overall body systems recover from training. If you push too hard, too long, your body will eventually break down. Always take at least one day off between training sessions. In addition, always take at least one or two minutes to rest between exercise sets. Certain training systems recommend that you take as little time as possible between sets to get the most out of your training; however, this technique is not recommended for young athletes.

WARM-UP EXERCISES

The purpose of the warm-up period is to prepare the body for more vigorous activity and reduce the chance of injury. A gradual warm-up period increases the blood flow to the muscles, which actually warms the muscles so they can function more effectively. The warm-up period consists of a light aerobic period followed by some flexibility exercises. The light aerobic period might consist of some light calisthenics, jogging in place, or 5 to 10 minutes on some stationary aerobic exercise equipment. Some suggested flexibility exercises are described in Chapter 4. An adequate warm-up period should last at least 10 minutes.

COOL-DOWN EXERCISES

The purpose of the cool-down period is to allow the body to gradually return to the resting state after exercise. The cool-down period basically consists of the same exercises as the warm-up period and should last between 10 and 15 minutes.

KEEP TRACK OF YOUR PROGRESS

It is important to keep track of your progress. After each workout, record the number of sets and repetitions performed. Also make notes about how you felt: Were you tired or rested? Did a particular exercise cause you more problems than others? Did you have a new pain? A training log will help you train smart. An example of a training log can be found in Appendix A.

KEY POINTS

- Virtually all strength and weight training programs are based on a variation of the fundamental principles of strength and weight training (load, repetition, intensity, rest, and frequency).
- Setting goals will help you achieve faster, safer, and more effective results.
- Periodization, or cycling, is a technique to help athletes vary the type, amount, and intensity of training for several weeks, a month, or a whole year.
- It is possible to develop significant levels of strength without any changes in muscle size.
- A split routine system trains different body parts on alternate days in an effort to stimulate hypertrophy of all muscles in a particular area of the body.
- With the superset system, opposing muscle groups are worked through exercises performed one right after another.
- A strength and weight training program for general conditioning should consist of two to three days of strength training, in addition to cardiovascular conditioning (running, swimming, cycling, etc.), for at least 30 to 40 minutes, three days per week.
- It is important to focus on the specific muscle groups utilized in a particular sport and develop your training program around exercises that will strengthen those muscle groups.
- Rest is needed between workouts to replace the energy stores in your muscles (glycogen) and to let your overall body systems recover from training.
- A gradual warm-up period increases the blood flow to the muscles, which actually warms the muscles so they can function more effectively.

Part II
Specific Strength and Weight Training Exercises

4

Flexibility Exercises

Three modes of flexibility training are commonly used: slow-sustained stretching, ballistic stretching, and proprioceptive neuromuscular facilitation (PNF) stretching. The technique most appropriate for use with young athletes is slow-sustained stretching. After a brief warm-up, both upper- and lower-body stretches should be performed before participating in any athletic activities. With the slow-sustained stretching technique, muscles are gradually lengthened through a joint's complete range of motion, held for a few seconds, and then released to the starting position. Ballistic stretching is a bouncing motion that may or may not be held for a brief period of time. It is the least effective and least safe form of stretching. PNF stretching uses a contraction-relaxation sequence to improve flexibility. With PNF, one muscle or group of muscles (e.g., quadriceps) is contracted, then there is a static stretch of the opposing muscle or muscle group (e.g., hamstrings).

FLEXIBILITY EXERCISES

LOWER-BODY EXERCISES
Supine Hamstring Stretch
Modified Hurdler's Stretch
Standing Quadriceps Stretch
Achilles Tendon and Calf Stretch

UPPER-BODY EXERCISES
Triceps Stretch
Shoulder and Chest Stretch
Rotator Cuff Stretch

Lower-Body Exercises
Supine Hamstring Stretch

Exercise Technique: Lie on your back on the floor and pull one leg to an upright stretched position. The leg should remain as straight as possible. The opposite leg is bent with the heel on the floor. Alternate legs.

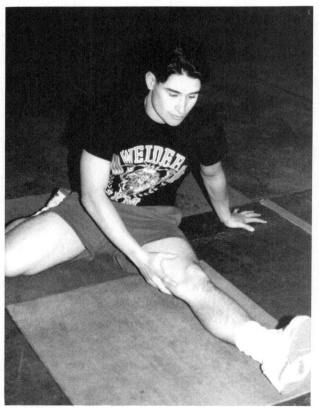

Supine Hamstring Stretch

Modified Hurdler's Stretch

Exercise Technique: Sit on the floor with one leg extended and the other leg bent and turned outward (heel against the thigh of the straight leg). Bend forward at the waist (leaning toward the straight leg) until a stretch is achieved, and then hold this position for the required count. Alternate legs.

Modified Hurdler's Stretch

Standing Quadriceps Stretch

Exercise Technique: You should be standing (and may be supported by another person or an object) and should grasp a leg by the ankle with the opposite arm. Pull the leg to a stretched position, taking care not to allow the knee to drift away from the side of the adjoining leg. Alternate legs.

Standing Quadriceps Stretch

Achilles Tendon and Calf Stretch

Exercise Technique: Face the wall and place both palms on the wall or place both hands on the waist. Place one foot 18 inches behind the other with both heels on the floor. Bend down and forward, keeping both heels on the floor until you accomplish a sufficient stretch.

Achilles Tendon and Calf Stretch

Triceps Stretch

Upper-Body Exercises
Triceps Stretch

Exercise Technique: With one hand, grasp the opposite elbow and pull the arm behind the head and down until you feel a stretch in the back of the arm. Hold for the desired time and repeat for the other arm.

Shoulder and Chest Stretch

Exercise Technique: Place one arm parallel to the floor and back behind the torso. You may hold onto a wall, partner, or whatever is available. To further improve the effectiveness of this stretch, turn away from the side being stretched until the stretch is felt in the shoulder and lateral chest region. Alternate sides.

Shoulder and Chest Stretch

Rotator Cuff Stretch

Rotator Cuff Stretch

Exercise Technique: For this stretch to be effective, you should grasp the elbow of the opposite arm (keeping it bent at a 90-degree angle) and pull it across the chest until you feel the stretch. Alternate arms.

5   Calisthenic Exercises

Calisthenic exercises are among the oldest forms of exercise. They use the weight of the body for the resistance. The resistance can be adjusted by changing body positions or by performing more repetitions. Calisthenic exercises are convenient because they do not require any assistance or any equipment. They are generally performed after a brief cardiovascular and stretching warm-up and can be performed before or after a cardiovascular workout. They can also be performed on alternating days from aerobic exercise or in conjunction with other forms of resistance exercises described throughout the book.

GENERAL GUIDELINES FOR PERFORMING CALISTHENIC EXERCISES

1. Always warm up before performing calisthenic exercises.
2. Remember to breathe evenly during the exercises.
3. Perform each exercise slowly, using controlled movements.
4. Support the lower back at all times.
5. Try and perform each exercise through a full range of motion.
6. As with many of the routines described in this chapter, always try and work the larger muscle groups first.

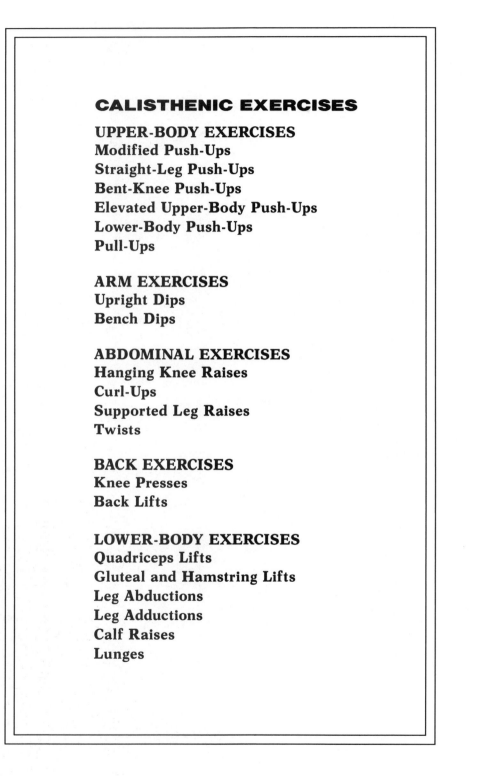

CALISTHENIC EXERCISES

UPPER-BODY EXERCISES
Modified Push-Ups
Straight-Leg Push-Ups
Bent-Knee Push-Ups
Elevated Upper-Body Push-Ups
Lower-Body Push-Ups
Pull-Ups

ARM EXERCISES
Upright Dips
Bench Dips

ABDOMINAL EXERCISES
Hanging Knee Raises
Curl-Ups
Supported Leg Raises
Twists

BACK EXERCISES
Knee Presses
Back Lifts

LOWER-BODY EXERCISES
Quadriceps Lifts
Gluteal and Hamstring Lifts
Leg Abductions
Leg Adductions
Calf Raises
Lunges

Upper-Body Exercises
Straight-Leg Push-Ups

Muscle Groups Worked: Pectoralis major (upper chest), anterior deltoid (front of top portion of the upper arm), triceps brachii (back of the upper arm)

Starting Position: Lie face down with body completely straight, legs close together, hands facing forward and shoulder-width apart, and head in a relaxed forward position.

Exercise Technique: Bend the elbows with a controlled motion, gradually lowering the body until the chest touches the floor. At this point, push away from the floor until the body is returned to the starting position. Keep the torso and legs straight throughout the motion.

Straight-Leg Push-Ups—
starting position

Straight-Leg Push-Ups—
finishing position

Bent-Knee Push-Ups

Muscle Groups Worked: Identical to those used in the straight-leg push-up

Starting Position: Lie face down with torso completely straight and arms placed shoulder-width apart. The knees are bent and in contact with the mat while the feet are close together. The weight of the body is distributed between the hands and the knees.

Exercise Technique: Bend the elbows and lower the body in a controlled manner until the chest touches the floor. At this point, push away from the floor until the starting position is regained.

Bent-Knee Push-Ups—starting position

Bent-Knee Push-Ups—finishing position

Elevated Upper-Body Push-Ups—starting position

Elevated Upper-Body Push-Ups— finishing position

Elevated Upper-Body Push-Ups

Muscle Groups Worked: Identical to those used in the previous two exercises with added emphasis on the anterior deltoid (front of top portion of the upper arm) and the sternal portion of the pectoralis major (center of the upper-chest area) *Starting Position:* Lie face down with body completely straight, legs close together, hands facing forward and shoulder-width apart on elevated bars (thumbs in), and head in a relaxed forward position. *Exercise Technique:* Bend the elbows and lower the body in a controlled manner until the chest touches the floor or you feel that you have reached the limits of your range of motion. At this point, push away from the bottom position until the starting position has been regained. *Safety and Spotting Techniques:* Use care in estimating the width of the bar spacing. A wider spacing will focus more on the chest muscles, while a narrower spacing will focus more on the arm muscles. Be certain, however, that you can handle the stresses associated with these varied placements. In addition, it is important to buy sturdy arm elevators to prevent slipping.

Lower-Body Push-Ups

Muscle Groups Worked: Identical to those used in previous push-up exercises with added emphasis on the anterior deltoid (front of top portion of upper arm) and the proximal portion of the pectoralis major (upper part of the chest muscles)
Starting Position: Lie face down with body completely straight, legs close together and elevated on a box (height 6 to 24 inches depending on the individual), hands facing forward and shoulder-width apart, and head in a relaxed forward position.
Exercise Technique: Bend the elbows and lower the body in a controlled manner until the chest touches the floor. Upon reaching this position, push away from the floor until the starting position is regained.
Safety and Spotting Techniques: Again it is important that you do not exceed your limits. The height of the box will be determined by your fitness (more advanced lifters will require a higher box). It is also important that the box is sturdy and placed on a nonslip surface.

Lower-Body Push-Ups

Pull-Ups—starting position

Pull-Ups—finishing position

Pull-Ups

Muscle Groups Worked: Deltoid and biceps brachii (top portion of upper arm), latissimus dorsi (major back muscle—middle and lower back)
Starting Position: Grasp bar with arms completely extended, torso straight, legs straight or bent, palms facing away from the body, and head in a relaxed position.
Exercise Technique: Pull upward with the arms and back until the chin clears the bar. At this point, lower in a controlled fashion until the starting position is regained. For variation, use a chinning grip (with palms facing the body) to involve the biceps brachii muscle.

Safety and Spotting Techniques: It is important that you do not cheat by kicking or jerking the body upward. If you need assistance, a spotter can place her or his hands on your waist (and lift up) or place the hands under your feet (allowing you to push off of the spotter's hands). Additional weight may be added around your waist through the use of belts made for this purpose. The use of various hand spacings varies the range of motion that you will work through; a wide spacing leads to a more narrow range of motion, while a shoulder-width spacing yields a greater range of motion.

Arm Exercises
Upright Dips

Muscle Groups Worked: Pectoralis major (chest area), triceps brachii (back of upper arm), deltoid (top portion of upper arm)

Starting Position: Keep body and legs completely straight (or legs bent if this position is more comfortable), grip the bars in line with the upper body (thumbs turned inward), and keep head in a relaxed forward position.

Exercise Technique: Bend the elbows lowering with a controlled motion until the elbows reach a 90-degree angle. At this point, push away from the bars while focusing on keeping the elbows in toward the torso to the greatest extent possible.

Safety and Spotting Techniques: It is important to avoid swaying or bouncing movements while performing this exercise. Leaning forward while executing this exercise throws more stress on the chest muscles, while remaining more upright stresses the back of the upper arms more completely. If you cannot complete a regular dip, you may still benefit from this exercise by jumping up to the starting position and concentrating only on lowering (doing negative repetitions).

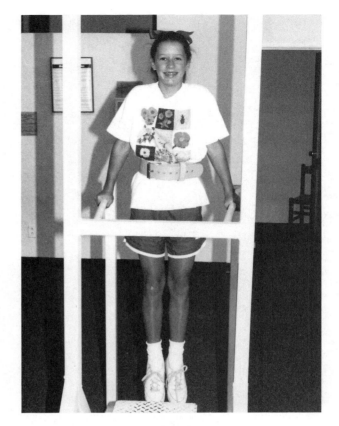

Upright Dips—starting position

Upright Dips—finishing position

Bench Dips

Muscle Groups Worked: Pectoralis major (chest muscle), deltoid (top portion of upper arm), triceps brachii (back of upper arm)

Starting Position: Begin with your heels resting on a raised surface (a bench, chair, etc.) and the hands on the edge of a bench. The hands are spaced slightly wider than shoulder width with the fingers pointing toward the torso. The legs are straight, and the hips are below the bench supporting the arms. The elbows are flexed at an angle approximating 90 degrees when supporting the upper body in this position.

Exercise Technique: Keep your heels stationary and your legs straight as you extend the elbows pushing the upper body up from the lower position. Continue pushing upward until the arms are extended.

Bench Dips—starting position

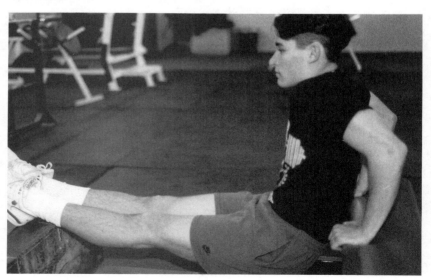

Bench Dips—finishing position

Abdominal Exercises
Hanging Knee Raises

Muscle Groups Worked: Rectus abdominis (front portion of torso from the chest to the hips), iliacus and psoas major (front portion of uppermost thigh)

Starting Position: Hang from the pull-up/chin bar with a shoulder-width grip facing away from the apparatus. The torso and legs are straight, and the head is facing forward.

Exercise Technique: Begin the movement by elevating the legs and bringing the knees in to the torso. To finish the movement, lower the legs in a controlled fashion to the starting position. The back and arms should remain relatively motionless throughout this movement. In addition, do not assist the muscles being worked by performing any swinging or jerking motions.

Hanging Knee Raises—starting position

Hanging Knee Raises—finishing position

Curl-Ups

Muscle Groups Worked: Rectus abdominis (front portion of torso from the chest to the hips)

Starting Position: Lie down with the knees bent and feet touching the floor; keep the torso straight, hands interlocked and supporting the head or arms crossed on the chest, head in a relaxed position.

Exercise Technique: Begin the movement by curling the spine upward and forward off the mat. Stop the movement when the shoulder blades leave the mat and you have curled up approximately 30 degrees.

At this point, slowly return to the original position.

Safety and Spotting Techniques: Take care not to pull the head up with the arms; the motion should originate in the abdominals. Always perform this exercise in a slow and controlled fashion. As always, if form breaks down and you must cheat to achieve more reps, stop exercising immediately. Advanced athletes may choose to do this exercise on an elevated board to achieve a higher exercise intensity.

Curl-Ups

Supported Leg Raises

Muscle Groups Worked: Rectus abdominis (front portion of the torso from the chest to the hips), iliacus and psoas major (front portion of uppermost thigh)
Starting Position: Lie on the ground with your hands under the gluteus for low-back support.
Exercise Technique: Raise both (or one leg at a time) legs into the air in a range from six to 24 inches off the ground.

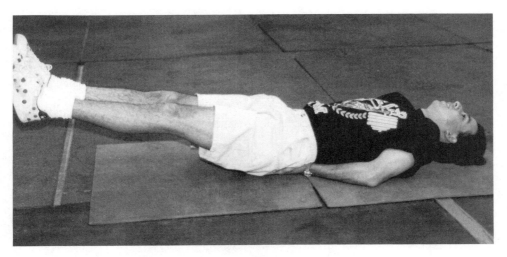

Supported Leg Raises—both legs

Supported Leg Raises—one leg

Twists

Muscle Groups Worked: Obliquus externus abdominis and obliquus internus abdominis (muscles on the side of the torso)

Starting Position: Sit on a bench with a dowel or broomstick held across the shoulders.

Exercise Technique: Twist from the starting position to a point where the right arm is directly in front of the face. Then return to the original position and follow up with a twist in which the left arm finishes in front of the face. Take care not to allow swinging or ballistic movement to occur; the movements should be controlled and precise.

Twists—right

Twists—left

Back Exercises
Knee Presses

Muscle Groups Worked: Gluteus maximus (buttocks), hamstring group (back of thigh), erector spinae group (muscles running from the low back to the neck area)

Starting Position: Kneel on the ground, supported on three limbs. Keep the head in the neutral position with one knee bent and held in by the chest.

Exercise Technique: Extend the bent knee backward as if kicking something behind you. The extension should be slow and controlled, not explosive. Be certain to work both sides of the body.

Knee Presses—
starting position

Knee Presses—
finishing position

Back Lifts

Muscle Groups Worked: Gluteus maximus (buttocks), hamstring group (back of the thigh), erector spinae group (muscles running from the low back to the neck area)

Starting Position: Lie down on the floor, face down. The arms should be outstretched above the head.

Exercise Technique: With control, raise the right arm and the left leg simultaneously as high as possible. After lowering, repeat this sequence with the left arm and right leg.

Back Lifts

Lower-Body Exercises
Quadriceps Lifts

Muscle Groups Worked: Quadriceps group: vastus lateralis, vastus intermedius, vastus medialis, rectus femoris (front of the thigh), illiacus and psoas major (uppermost portion of thigh)

Starting Position: Lie on your back with both arms alongside the body. Bend the leg that is not being exercised with the heel flat on the floor. Straighten the other leg and flex the ankle.

Exercise Technique: Raise the leg off the floor until you reach the limit of the range of motion. When finished with the exercise on one side, alternate legs.

Quadriceps Lifts
(Same position as for
Supported Leg Raises
on page 48.)

Gluteal and Hamstring Lifts

Muscle Groups Worked: Gluteus maximus (buttocks), hamstring group: biceps femoris, semitendinosus, semimembranosus (back of the thigh)
Starting Position: Kneel on the floor with the support of all four limbs. Bend the knee of the exercising leg with the calf lifted off the floor.

Exercise Technique: Raise the bent knee up until the thigh is parallel to the floor. At this point, extend the leg backward until it is straight. Return the knee to the floor to start the second repetition. When one side has been exercised, switch to the other leg.

Gluteal and Hamstring Lifts—starting position

Gluteal and Hamstring Lifts—finishing position

Leg Abductions

Muscle Groups Worked: Gluteus medius, gluteus minimus, tensor fasciae latae (lateral thigh and outer hip muscles)
Starting Position: Rest on your right forearm and hip. Bend the bottom leg at a 90-degree angle. Keep the top leg straight and lying over the bottom leg with the ankle flexed.

Exercise Technique: From this position, raise the straight leg until you reach the limit of the range of motion. Reverse this procedure for the other side. Keep the back erect throughout this motion.

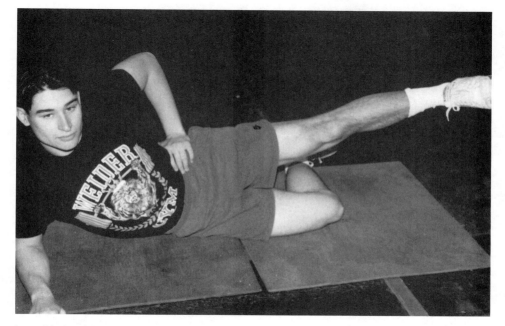

Leg Abductions

Leg Adductions

Muscle Groups Worked: Adductor magnus, adductor brevis, adductor longus, pectineus, gracilis (muscles on the inside of the thigh)

Leg Adductions—starting position

Starting Position: Lie on your back with arms by your side. Lift the legs to form a *V* and separate them as widely as possible. *Exercise Technique:* Bring the legs together from the extended *V* position until they meet in the vertical position.

Leg Adductions—finishing position

Calf Raises

Muscle Groups Worked: Gastrocnemius, soleus (calf muscles)

Starting Position: Stand on one leg on a step and grasp the railing. The ball of the foot is on the step and the heel of that foot is hanging below the step. The other foot is wrapped around the back of the ankle.

Exercise Technique: Go up on your toes until you reach complete extension, and then go down again into the starting position. Reverse the leg positioning to work the other leg.

Calf Raises

Lunges

Muscle Groups Worked: Quadriceps group (front thigh muscle), hamstring group (back of thigh), gluteus maximus (buttocks)

Starting Position: Stand upright with the hands on the hips. Keep the legs approximately shoulder-width apart.

Exercise Technique: Step forward until the thigh and calf muscle describe a 90-degree angle. Then push away from the floor until the upright position is regained. Use the same procedure for the opposite leg.

Lunges—starting position

Lunges—finishing position

6   Tubing Resistance Exercises

Another safe, inexpensive, and effective way for young athletes to develop strength is with the use of rubber tubing. The rubber tubing provides resistance during the exercise movements. Tubing comes in different lengths and tensions so that young athletes of different ages and abilities can exercise safely and effectively.

GENERAL GUIDELINES FOR USING EXERCISE BANDS AND TUBING

1. Before using any tubing, always check for tears, cuts, or abnormal wear and tear points.
2. Perform each exercise as illustrated. Perform the extension on a slow count of one, two, and return on three, four.
3. On the return, the rubber tubing should never go completely slack. Always maintain slight tension.
4. The appropriate tension of tubing should allow you to complete a minimum of 10 repetitions.

5. Increase repetitions to 20 before considering a resistance increase.
6. For certain large muscle group exercises, increase the resistance by doubling up the tubing.
7. Always make sure the tubing is centered under the shoe.
8. Most resistance training with rubber tubing is designed for high repetition and moderate resistance. This minimizes chances of muscle overload, strain, or "snapping back."
9. Understand that rubber exercise tubing is not a toy.
10. Keep your face turned slightly away from the direction of the exercise movement.
11. Always control the tubing during the return phase of the exercise movement.
12. If unable to complete an exercise for at least 10 repetitions with correct technique, use a lighter resistance.
13. Always follow the recommendations of the manufacturer.

TUBING RESISTANCE EXERCISES

UPPER-BODY EXERCISES
Seated Shoulder Presses
Standing Chest Presses
Upright Rows
One-Arm Press-Outs
Lat Pull-Downs
Side Bends
Push-Ups
Seated Rows

ARM EXERCISES
Triceps Extensions
Biceps Curls
Wrist Curls

LOWER-BODY EXERCISES
Squats
Hip Abductions
Hip Flexions
Leg Curls
Calf Raises

Upper-Body Exercises
Seated Shoulder Presses

Muscle Groups Worked: Deltoid (front part of upper arm), triceps and anconeus (back of upper arm)

Starting Position: Sit on a bench with the tubing under the gluteus muscles. Bend the elbows at a 90-degree angle, the palms facing away from the body while grasping the handles.

Exercise Technique: Push up on the handles until the arms are completely extended. Exercise caution in avoiding back arching while performing this exercise.

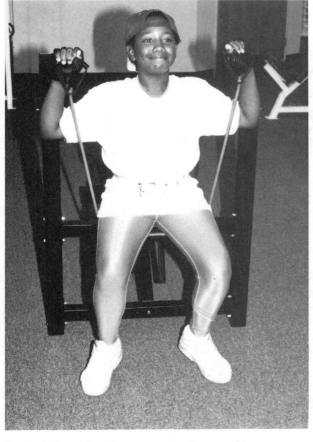

Seated Shoulder Presses—starting position

Seated Shoulder Presses—finishing position

Standing Chest Presses

Muscle Groups Worked: Pectoralis major (chest muscle), deltoid (front part of upper arm and shoulder), triceps (back of upper arm)

Starting Position: Stand with feet comfortably apart and the tubing wrapped around the shoulder area. The palms are facing down and grasping the handles.

Exercise Technique: Press the arms away from the body until you reach the extended position. As always, it is important that you avoid any jerking movements or back arching.

Standing Chest Presses—starting position

Standing Chest Presses—finishing position

Upright Rows—starting position

Upright Rows—finishing position

Upright Rows

Muscle Groups Worked: Deltoid and biceps brachii (front part of upper arm and shoulder), trapezius (largest muscle of the upper-back and lower-neck area)
Starting Position: Stand (with the tubing under the midshoe area) with the feet together and the toes pointing straight ahead. Arms are hanging by the torso with the palms facing the body while grasping the handles of the tubing.

Exercise Technique: Pull the handles upward toward the body until the hands reach a position under the chin. The elbows are to the side and rise with the hands, finishing in a slightly higher position.

One-Arm Press-Outs

Muscle Groups Worked: Pectoralis major (chest muscle), deltoid (front part of upper arm and shoulder), triceps and anconeus (back of upper arm)

Starting Position: Take a shoulder-width stance and hold the tubing close to the chest with the arm that will be exercised for that set. The other arm is extended straight out with the palm facing away and holding the tubing (which may be doubled if necessary to shorten the length).

Exercise Technique: Pull away from the body with the exercising arm until the tubing is tight. Simultaneously, have the opposite arm resist the pull. When one set is completed, switch sides and repeat the procedure.

One-Arm Press-Outs—starting position

One-Arm Press-Outs—finishing position

Lat Pull-Downs

Muscle Groups Worked: Triceps (back of upper arm), trapezius (largest muscle of the upper-back and neck area), latissimus dorsi (major back muscle—middle and lower back)

Starting Position: Take a shoulder-width stance and hold the tubing overhead with arms completely extended. The arms are out about six inches wider than the shoulders on either side of the body. Do not attempt to grip both ends of the tubing; instead take a section that affords sufficient resistance.

Exercise Technique: Remain upright as you pull the arms down to a position where the arms are parallel to the floor. Focus on pulling the shoulder blades together in this motion and keeping the arms in line with the body.

Lat Pull-Downs—starting position

Lat Pull-Downs—finishing position

Side Bends

Muscle Groups Worked: Obliquus externus abdominus, obliquus internus abdominus (muscles on the side of the mid- and lower torso)

Starting Position: Stand on the tubing (which is bent in half) with the handles both held on one side of the torso. Incline the body to either the left or right as far as you can comfortably extend.

Exercise Technique: From the side bending position previously described, take the torso back to an upright position. Make sure to work both sides of the body.

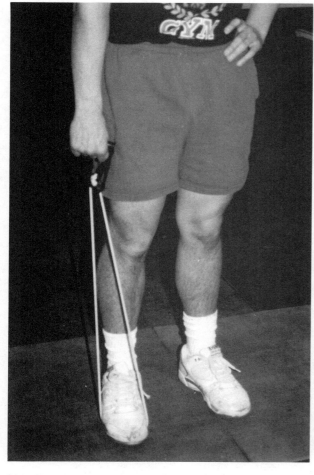

Side Bends—starting position

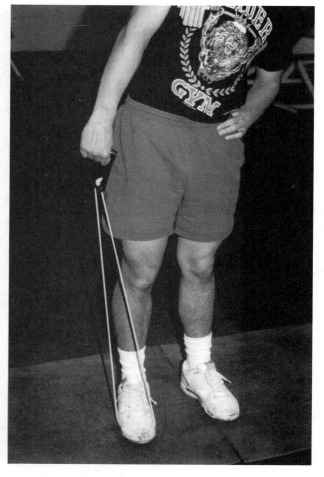

Side Bends—finishing position

Push-Ups

Muscle Groups Worked: Pectoralis major (chest muscle), deltoid (front part of upper arm and shoulder), triceps and anconeus (back of upper arm)

Starting Position: Support yourself approximately six inches from the floor with the body and legs straightened. The hands are about shoulder-width apart, and each hand is over one end of the tubing, which runs over the back and is tightly stretched.

Exercise Technique: From this point, push away from the floor exactly as you would in a normal push up (with the tubing resisting the upward push).

Push-Ups

Seated Rows

Muscle Groups Worked: Trapezius and latissimus muscles (upper back muscles) and biceps brachii (upper front part of arm)

Starting Position: While seated, place the legs straight, knees bent slightly, and feet together. Place the middle of the tubing around the feet, and grab both ends of the tubing.

Exercise Technique: Keep the back straight and chin tucked. Bend the elbows and bring the thumbs toward the shoulders. Return slowly to the starting position.

Arm Exercises
Triceps Extensions

Muscle Groups Worked: Triceps and anconeus (back of upper arm)
Starting Position: Sit on a bench with the tubing firmly underneath the buttocks. One handle is in each hand with the palms facing the ceiling and the hands behind the head. The elbows are bent at a 90-degree angle.

Exercise Technique: Extend the lower arm upward while keeping the elbows stationary. As always the tubing should be taut at the beginning of this exercise to insure sufficient resistance.

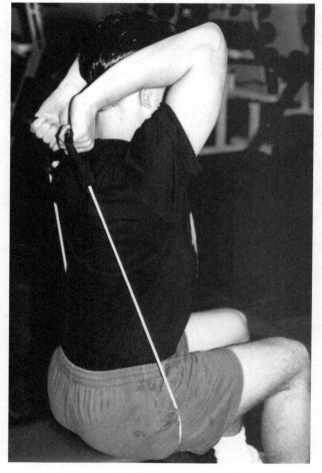

Triceps Extensions—starting position

Triceps Extensions—finishing position

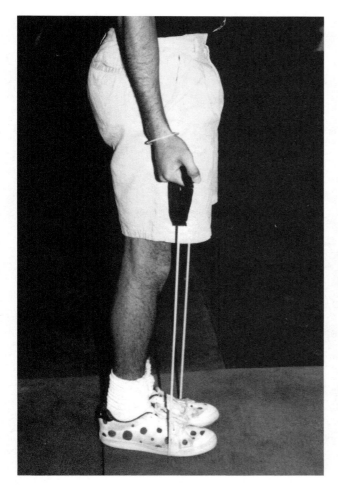

Biceps Curls—starting position

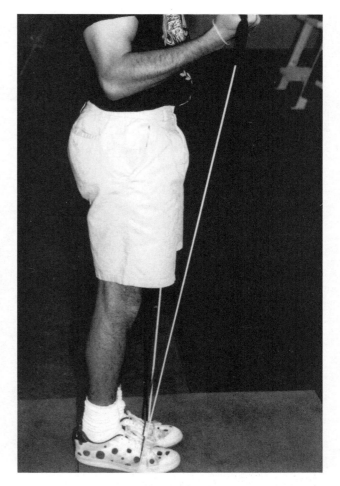

Biceps Curls—finishing position

Biceps Curls

Muscle Groups Worked: Biceps brachii
and brachioradialis (front of upper arm)
Starting Position: Stand on the tubing with
the feet together and facing forward. The
palms are facing away from the torso
(with the arms extended) and grasping the
handles.

Exercise Technique: Pull the handles
toward the torso while keeping the elbows
stationary. Attempt to pull with a smooth,
controlled motion and avoid jerking or
arching of the back.

Wrist Curls

Muscle Groups Worked: Flexor carpi radialis, flexor carpi ulnaris (forearm muscles on the palm side)

Starting Position: Have forearms resting on a bench with the hands hanging over the edge grasping the tubing handles. The end of the tubing is taut and secured under the bench. Kneel by the bench.

Exercise Technique: Pull the handles toward the torso. With the forearms staying in contact with the bench, the forearm muscles are exercised.

Wrist Curls—starting position

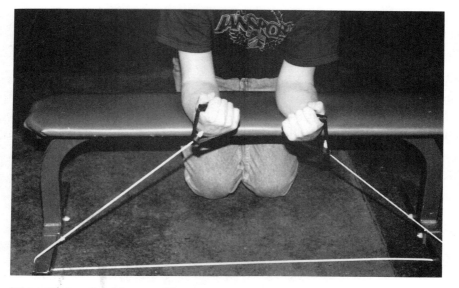

Wrist Curls—finishing position

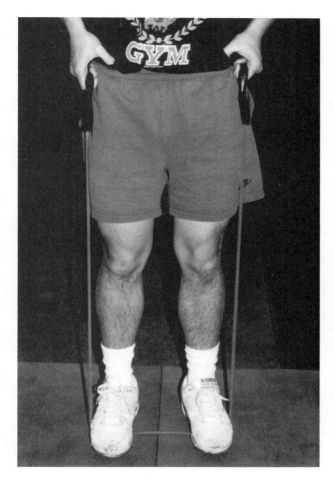

Squats—starting position

Squats—finishing position

Lower-Body Exercises
Squats

Muscle Groups Worked: Gluteus maximus (butt muscle), quadriceps group (front of thighs), hamstring group (back of thighs), erector spinae group (low-back area), gastrocnemius, and soleus (calf muscles)

Starting Position: Stand (with the tubing under the midshoe area) with the feet shoulder-width apart and toes pointing slightly outward. The knees are bent at an angle of 90 degrees, and the thigh is inclined slightly forward, but it is straight. Hold the handles at about hip level.

Exercise Technique: Push away from the floor with the legs until you reach the upright position. Keep the hands motionless throughout the exercise. As you push up, focus on keeping the back straight, looking forward, and on not rounding the shoulders.

Hip Abductions

Muscle Groups Worked: Gluteus medius, gluteus minimus, tensor fasciae latae (muscles on the outer side of the thigh and hip)

Starting Position: Lie on your side with the tubing wrapped tightly around the ankle area and anchored by the leg closest to the floor. One hand may be used to support the head while this exercise is performed.

Exercise Technique: From this position, lift the leg away from the other leg until you reach the limit of the range of motion. Be certain to work both sides.

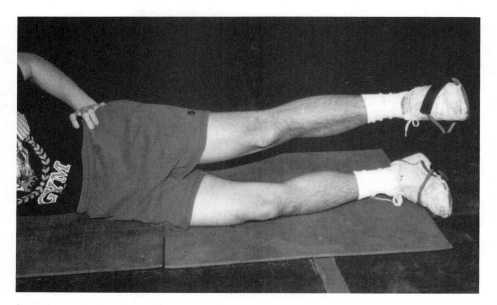

Hip Abductions

Hip Flexions

Muscle Groups Worked: Psoas major, illiacus (muscles on the extreme upper thigh and lower side groin area)

Starting Position: Lie on the back with both arms alongside the body and both legs straight. The leg that will be exercised has the tubing over the upper part of the ball of the foot (which is flexed to prevent slipping). The tubing is either held by a partner or anchored under something heavy and immovable.

Exercise Technique: Pull the knee of the leg with the tubing on it toward the torso until the limit of the range of motion is reached. Your back must remain flat throughout the exercise. Be certain to work both sides.

Hip Flexions

Leg Curls

Muscle Groups Worked: Hamstring group (back of thigh area)

Starting Position: Lie on the floor, face down, legs straight. Secure the tubing around your ankles. The spotter is positioned behind you holding the handles of the tubing.

Exercise Technique: Pull the heels toward the buttocks, while keeping the thigh in contact with the floor. The spotter resists by pulling against this upward motion.

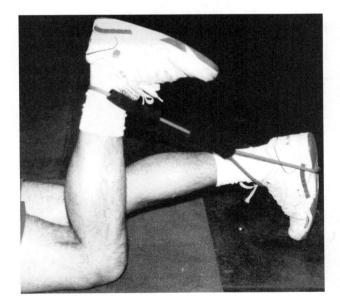

Leg Curls

Calf Raises

Muscle Groups Worked: Gastrocnemius and soleus (calf muscles)
Starting Position: Stand (flat-footed) with both feet on ends of the tubing. The tubing should be under the balls of the feet and draped over your shoulders.
Exercise Technique: Go up on the balls of your feet, driving up against the resistance of the tubing.

Calf Raises—starting position

Calf Raises—finishing position

7   Manual Resistance Exercises

Manual resistance exercises use cooperative efforts between partners to develop strength. They are an ideal substitute for conventional resistance training routines. In manual resistance strength training no equipment is required, many different muscle groups can be worked, and the speed of the movements can be controlled. If a variety of equipment is available, manual resistance can be used to supplement a workout. Manual resistance exercises can add variety to a workout and significantly increase the number of exercises available to the young athlete.

GENERAL GUIDELINES FOR PERFORMING MANUAL RESISTANCE EXERCISES

1. The lifter and spotter need to communicate before, during, and after each exercise.
2. The spotter should try and keep equal amounts of tension applied to the muscles being exercised.
3. The lifter should pause momentarily in the fully contracted position.
4. Maximum resistance should not be applied during the first few repetitions.
5. The spotter may need to vary the resistance during the lifting and the lowering phases.
6. The lifter and spotter should make every effort to make sure the transition from the raising to the lowering phase is done smoothly.
7. Both upper- and lower-body routines can and should be performed.

MANUAL RESISTANCE EXERCISES

UPPER-BODY EXERCISES
Push-Ups
Side Lateral Raises
Butterflyes
Bent-Over Side Lateral Raises
Shoulder Presses
One-Arm Rows

ARM EXERCISES
French Curls
Biceps Curls

ABDOMINAL EXERCISES
Curl-Ups
Leg Raises

LOWER-BODY EXERCISES
Leg Abductions
Hip Flexions
Knee Flexions
Leg Curls
Ankle Plantar- and Dorsiflexions
Foot Inversions and Eversions

NECK EXERCISES
Neck Flexions
Neck Extensions
Shoulder Shrugs

Upper-Body Exercises
Push-Ups

Muscle Groups Worked: Pectoralis major (chest muscle), deltoid (front part of upper arm and shoulder), triceps and anconeus (back of upper arm)

Starting Position: Lifter: start with the torso and legs straight and the hands shoulder-width apart. The chest is touching the ground and the fingers are pointing away from the body in a parallel direction.

Spotter: straddle the lifter with the hands placed on the shoulder-blade (scapulae) or lower-back area for resistance.

Exercise Technique: Lifter: push away from the ground while maintaining a straight body position.

Spotter: apply resistance from above.

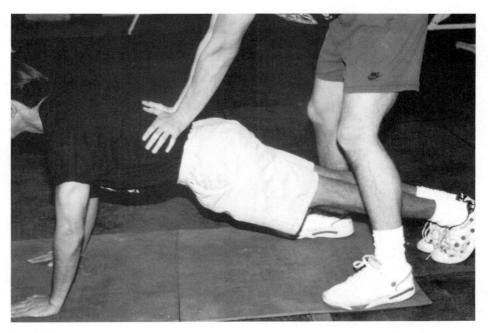

Push-Ups

Side Lateral Raises

Muscle Groups Worked: Deltoid (front part of upper arm)
Starting Position: Lifter: start with arms in the downward position, arms next to the torso.

Spotter: stand behind the lifter with your hands placed on the lifter's wrists.
Exercise Technique: Lifter: elevate the arms until the horizontal position is attained.

Spotter: give a sufficient level of manual resistance.

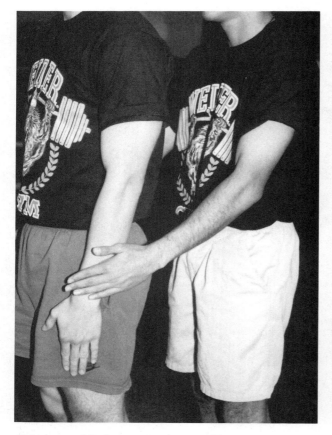

Side Lateral Raises—starting position

Side Lateral Raises—finishing position

Butterflyes

Muscle Groups Worked: Pectoralis major (chest muscle), deltoid (front part of upper arm), serratus anterior (side portion of upper chest)

Starting Position: Lifter: lie on your back with the knees bent and the arms bent at a 90-degree angle with the hands up and away from the body.

Spotter: place your hands on the inside of the lifter's elbows for the first part of the movement and on the outside of the elbows for the second part of the movement.

Exercise Technique: Lifter: pull both elbows in toward the midline of the body and then push back out. It is important that you focus on "squeezing the pecs" throughout the range of motion.

Spotter: apply pressure at the elbows.

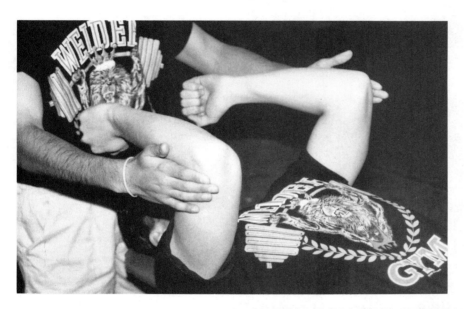

Butterflyes—Abduction

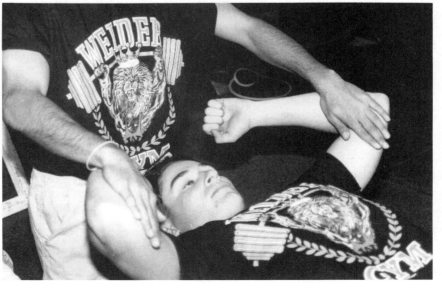

Butterflyes—Adduction

Bent-Over Side Lateral Raises—starting position

Bent-Over Side Lateral Raises—finishing position

Bent-Over Side Lateral Raises

Muscle Groups Worked: Posterior deltoid (back of shoulder musculature)

Starting Position: Lifter: stand with the torso inclined forward at an angle approximating 30 to 45 degrees and the arms down and along the side of the torso.

Spotter: stand facing the lifter and place your hands on the lifter's wrists.

Exercise Technique: Lifter: elevate the arms to a position where they are even with the shoulder area.

Spotter: apply resistance to counteract this movement.

Shoulder Presses

Muscle Groups Worked: Deltoid (front part of upper arm), triceps and anconeus (back of upper arm)

Starting Position: Lifter: sit on the floor in a comfortable position. Flex the arms at a 90-degree angle with the palms facing the ceiling.

Spotter: stand behind the lifter with your hands pressing down on the lifter's palms.

Exercise Technique: Lifter: push the arms upward.

Spotter: resist this motion with a downward pushing action. It is important that you do not resist too much, causing the lifter to arch the back while performing this exercise.

Shoulder Presses—
starting position

Shoulder Presses—
finishing position

One-Arm Rows

Muscle Groups Worked: Trapezius (largest muscle of upper-back and neck area), latissimus dorsi (major back muscle—middle and lower back), posterior deltoid (back of shoulder musculature)

Starting Position: Lifter: kneel on a bench with the back straight. The nonexercising arm is braced on the bench for support, and the other arm is hanging straight at the side.

Spotter: stand to the side of the arm to be worked and place both hands on the lifter's upper-arm area.

Exercise Technique: Lifter: drive the arm upward (leading with the elbow) to a position where the upper arm is parallel with the torso.

Spotter: apply resistance in a downward motion on the upper arm.

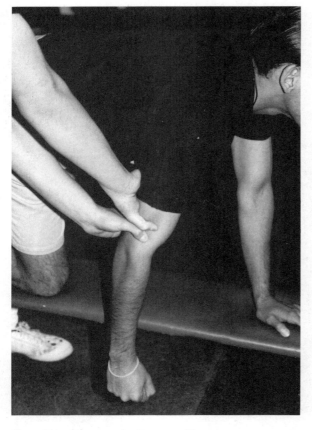

One-Arm Rows—starting position

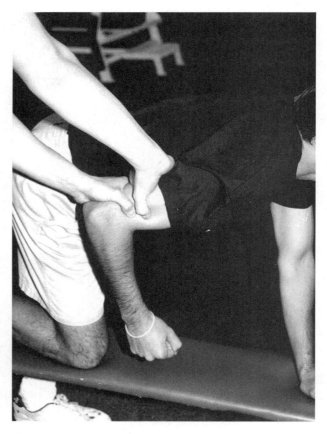

One-Arm Rows—finishing position

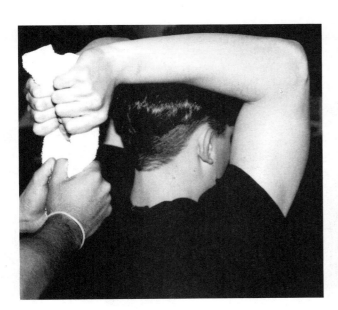

French Curls—starting position

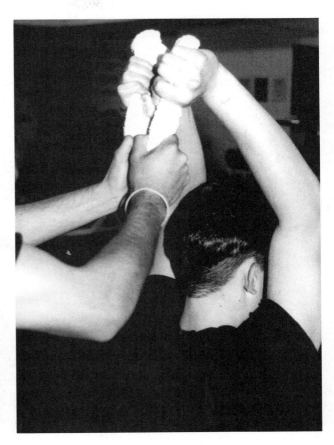

French Curls—finishing position

Arm Exercises
French Curls

Muscle Groups Worked: Triceps and anconeus (back of upper arm)

Starting Position: Lifter: sit on the edge of a bench facing away from the spotter, who is behind you. Have the elbows lifted high above the head and the hands grasping the middle of a towel down near the base of the skull.

Spotter: hold the ends of the towel.

Exercise Technique: Lifter: extend the lower arms up and away from the base of the skull to the fully extended position, while attempting to keep the elbows motionless throughout the exercise.

Spotter: maintain constant resistance in a manner that facilitates the lifter's execution of the exercise with correct technique.

Biceps Curls

Muscle Groups Worked: Biceps brachii and brachioradialis (front of upper arm)
Starting Position: Lifter: sit at the edge of a bench or chair. Extend the arms down between the legs while grasping the middle of a towel.

Spotter: kneel on the floor in front of the lifter and hold the ends of the towel.
Exercise Technique: Lifter: pull the arms upward toward the torso while keeping the elbows stationary.

Spotter: resist by pulling downward against the pull of the lifter.

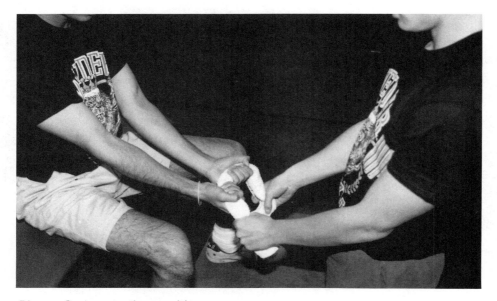

Biceps Curls—starting position

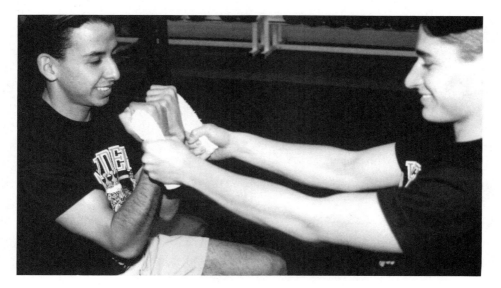

Biceps Curls—finishing position

Abdominal Exercises
Curl-Ups

Muscle Groups Worked: Rectus abdominus (muscle in front of the abdominal wall)

Starting Position: Lifter: lie on the floor with knees bent and the heels flat on the floor. Cross the arms over the chest.

Spotter: straddle the lifter to provide resistance in the center of the crossed arms.

Exercise Technique: Lifter: from the lying position, curl the upper body upward until the elbows contact the knees. Be cautious not to lift the lower back off the floor or to jerk the body upward.

Spotter: resist the motion.

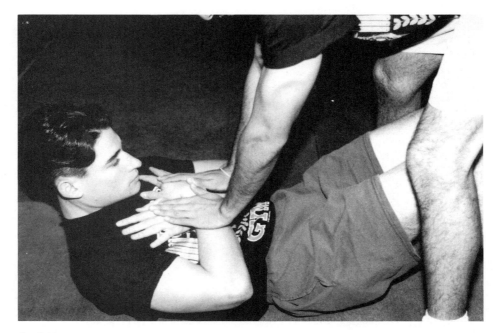

Curl-Ups

Leg Raises

Muscle Groups Worked: Rectus abdominus (muscle in front of the abdominal wall), psoas major and illiacus (upper part of thigh and lower lateral quadrant of groin area)

Starting Position: Lifter: lie flat on your back on the floor with the hands tucked under the buttocks for low-back area support.

Spotter: kneel along the side of the leg being exercised and be prepared to give resistance to the top of the thigh region.

Exercise Technique: Lifter: pull the leg (one side at a time) toward the upper body, stopping at a predetermined point. This point can be as low as 6 to 10 inches off the ground or as high as the point where the leg describes a 90-degree angle to the floor.

Spotter: resist the motion.

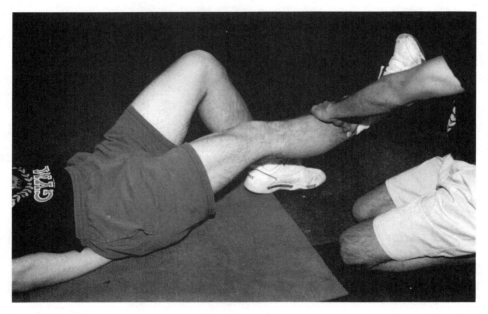

Leg Raises

Lower-Body Exercises
Leg Abductions

Muscle Groups Worked: Gluteus medius and minimus (upper lateral hip region) and tensor fasciae latae (lateral thigh area)

Starting Position: Lifter: lie on your side on the floor with the leg to be exercised on the top.

Spotter: sit behind the lifter and place both hands on the ankle region.

Exercise Technique: Lifter: elevate the leg away from the floor to the limit of the range of motion. Spotter: apply the appropriate pressure—enough to allow the lifter to fall in the prescribed repetition range for a given exercise.

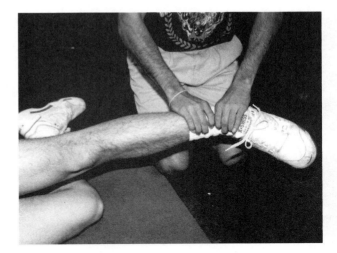

Leg Abductions

Hip Flexions

Muscle Groups Worked: Illiacus and psoas major (uppermost portion of upper thigh)

Starting Position: Lifter: lie flat on the back with legs together.

Spotter: sit on the side of the leg being exercised with both hands placed on the thigh area.

Exercise Technique: Lifter: pull the thigh upward toward the torso.

Spotter: resist this movement.

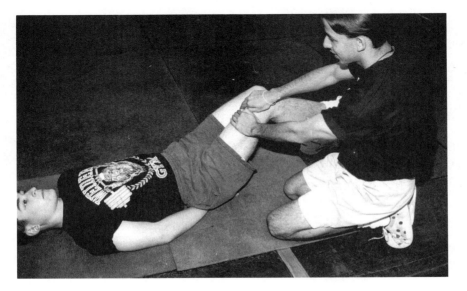

Hip Flexions

Knee Flexions

Muscle Groups Worked: Hamstring group: biceps femoris, semimembranosus, and semitendinosus (back of thigh)

Starting Position: Lifter: sit on the edge of the bench.

Spotter: sit behind the lifter and on the side to be exercised with both hands on the ankle or calf area.

Exercise Technique: Lifter: pull your heel toward the back of the thigh as the spotter resists. Avoid lifting the hips away from the floor as the exercise becomes difficult.

Spotter: resist the motion.

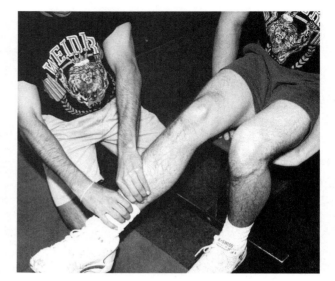

Knee Flexions

Leg Curls

Muscle Groups Worked: Hamstring group (back of upper-thigh area)

Starting Position: Lifter: lie on your stomach on the floor, with both legs straight. You may place the arms under the head for comfort.

Spotter: kneel at the feet of the lifter with both hands grasping the lifter's ankle.

Exercise Technique: Lifter: bring the lower leg up to a position of 90 degrees against downward resistance. The upper thigh must not break contact with the floor.

Spotter: resist the motion.

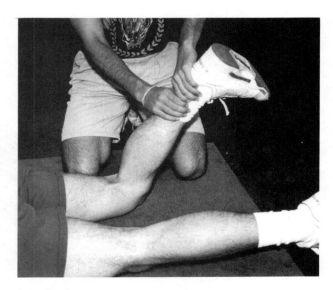

Leg Curls

Ankle Plantar- and Dorsiflexions

Muscle Groups Worked: Plantarflexion: gastrocnemius and soleus (calf muscles); dorsiflexion: tibialis anterior (front lateral portion of shin area)

Starting Position: Plantarflexion—Lifter: sit on the floor. Feet should be at a 90-degree angle.

Spotter: sit directly opposite the lifter with both hands on the underside of the lifter's feet.

Dorsiflexion—Lifter: sit on the floor with feet pointed toward the spotter.

Spotter: sit directly opposite the lifter with both hands on the top of the lifter's feet.

Exercise Technique: Plantarflexion—Lifter: push the feet away from the leg into a pointing position.

Spotter: resist the motion.

Dorsiflexion—Lifter: pull the feet toward the leg.

Spotter: resist the motion.

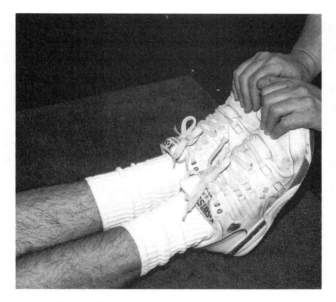

Ankle Plantarflexions

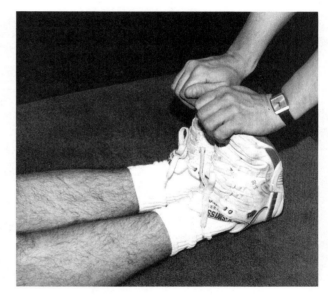

Ankle Dorsiflexions

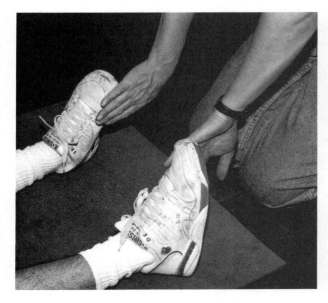

Foot Inversions

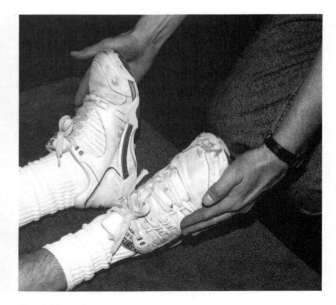

Foot Eversions

Foot Inversions and Eversions

Muscle Groups Worked: Inversion: tibialis posterior (muscle deeply located in the back of the calf); eversion: peroneus longus and peroneus brevis (lateral portion of calf and ankle area)

Starting Position: Inversion—Lifter: sit, preferably on an elevated surface. Keep feet in a neutral position (90-degree angle).

Spotter: place both hands under the ankles of the feet to be exercised.

Eversion—Lifter: sit on an elevated surface with the feet in neutral position.

Spotter: place both hands under the shin area.

Exercise Technique: Inversion—Lifter: pull the feet from the neutral position inward, turning the base of the feet upward in this movement.

Spotter: resist the motion.

Eversion—Lifter: pull the feet from the neutral position outward, keeping the base of the feet flat throughout the movement.

Spotter: note that in both of these exercises you should use caution in the amount of resistance given, as this area is not a strong one relative to other areas already mentioned.

Neck Exercises

Neck Flexions

Muscle Groups Worked:
Sternocleidomastoideus (major muscle on the side of the neck)

Starting Position: Lifter: lie on the back with the arms by the side.

Spotter: kneel by the lifter and place one hand on the abdominals to stabilize the lifter. The other hand is on the lifter's forehead.

Exercise Technique: Lifter: flex the neck region toward the torso against the spotter's resistance.

Spotter: resist the motion.

Neck Extensions

Muscle Groups Worked: Trapezius (largest muscle of upper-back and neck area), semispinalis capitis, splenius capitus, splenius cervicus (neck and upper-shoulder area muscles)

Starting Position: Lifter: lie on your stomach on an elevated bench with the neck area extended over the end of the bench.

Spotter: place both hands on the base of the back of the skull.

Exercise Technique: Lifter: extend your neck backward against resistance. Exercise caution on both neck exercises so that you do not force the range of motion.

Spotter: be careful in listening to the lifter in respect to how much force is applied.

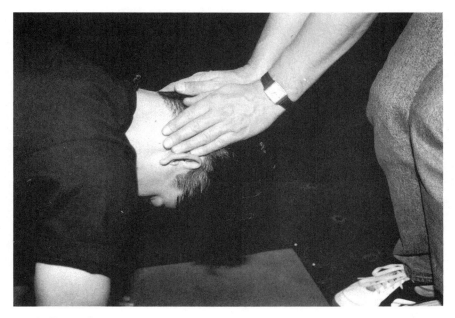

Neck Extensions

Shoulder Shrugs

Muscle Groups Worked: Trapezius (largest muscle of upper-back and neck area)
Starting Position: Lifter: sit on a bench.

Spotter: stand directly behind the lifter. Place both hands on the top of the lifter's shoulders for resistance.
Exercise Technique: Lifter: elevate or shrug the shoulders upward, attempting to touch the deltoid muscles to the ears, against the spotter's efforts.

Spotter: resist the motion.

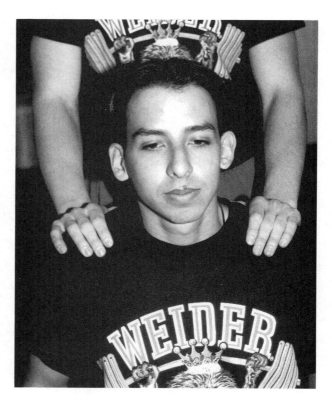

Shoulder Shrugs

8   Free Weights and Weight Machines

Working out with weights and weight machines is the most common form of strength training. Training with weights becomes safer and more effective as young athletes develop physically. This type of training can significantly improve an athlete's ability to perform in selected athletic events. In most cases, it is not recommended that children under the age of 12 lift free weights. Some children will mature faster, however, and weight lifting might be appropriate for some children under the age of 12. The United States Weight and Power Lifting Federation recommends that young children not lift maximal weights until the age of 14. Other experts recommend athletes not lift maximal weights until the age of 16. Practical considerations as to when an athlete can start lifting weights might include appropriate health, goals for lifting weights, coachability, and emotional maturity.

GENERAL GUIDELINES FOR TRAINING WITH WEIGHTS

1. Never exercise unsupervised.
2. Always use collars on barbells and dumbbells.
3. Never perform one-repetition maximum lifts.
4. Always breathe out during the explosive part of the lift.
5. Always use proper form and technique.
6. All lifting motions should be slow and controlled. Avoid fast or jerking motions.
7. Keep weights as close to your body as possible.
8. Lift with your knees and keep your back straight when picking up a weight from the ground.
9. Rest between exercises.
10. Lift with individual goals in mind.

CHOOSING THE CORRECT STARTING WEIGHT

When first performing an exercise, the correct starting weight must be established. Although there are a variety of ways to do this, the easiest and safest way is to have the athlete start out by performing an exercise 10 to 12 times. If that weight can be lifted without a great deal of exertion or fatigue, the weight is light enough to start with. This method of establishing the starting weight will be referred to as the ten-repetition maximum (10RM) method. The initial starting weight should be changed if chronic fatigue is noticed one to two days later.

WEIGHT TRAINING MACHINES

Most weight training machines were not designed for use by children. Although weight training machines can be safer than free weights, most children should not use equipment designed for adults. Some types of weight lifting equipment use stacks of weights, usually in 10-pound increments. If a 10-pound increase in weight is too much, another exercise should be performed until the athlete can safely lift the weight. Some young athletes may be able to fit on some weight training machines, but may not be able to lift the minimum weight. Again, in such cases, alternative exercises should be performed. If you cannot adapt a weight training machine to fit a child, an alternative exercise should be recommended. When in doubt, check the manufacturers' weight and height minimums for their equipment. For more information on weight training equipment specifically designed for children and young athletes, see Appendix D.

FREE-WEIGHT EQUIPMENT

Free-weight equipment, unlike weight training machines, can be safely used by young children. Every effort should be made to fit the child to the equipment. When purchasing weight training equipment, make sure it is made from heavy gauge steel. Always check the equipment for wear and tear or any defects. Young athletes should not use, or be around, free-weight training equipment without proper supervision.

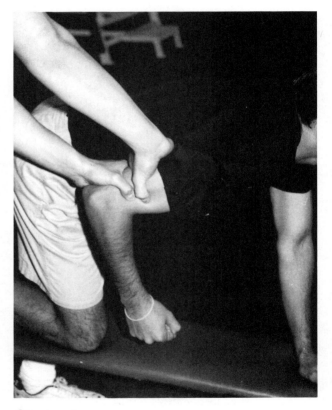

Squat rack

OTHER EQUIPMENT NEEDS

- *Shoes.* There are specially designed weight lifting shoes which provide extra foot support when lifting heavy weights. In most cases, a good pair of high-top or cross-training shoes will do fine.

Dumbbells

Barbells

- *Gloves.* Weight lifting gloves are highly recommended. Gloves help prevent blisters and help provide additional gripping support when lifting a barbell or dumbbells.
- *Wraps.* Wraps are elastic bandages that are wrapped around joints (typically knee joints) to provide additional support. Most beginning weight lifters and young athletes will not need to wear knee wraps. However, grip wraps, which are wrapped around the wrist and then the barbell, may be helpful.
- *Belts.* Weight training belts help provide support for the lower back. They come in various sizes and shapes. A weight training belt is not an absolute requirement, but it is particularly important to wear one when performing squats.

WEIGHT LIFTING SAFETY

The risk of injuries to children participating in weight training programs is low. However, injuries can occur in any sport or strenuous physical activity. To minimize the risk of injury during weight training, young athletes should follow these guidelines:

1. *Get medical clearance.* Prior to participating in a weight training program, you should have a medical examination by a physician knowledgeable in sports medicine.
2. *Workout only with proper supervision.* Proper supervision is perhaps the most important variable in reducing potential injuries. Not only must the supervisor be responsible for the overall safety of the weight training area, but he or she must also possess sufficient knowledge to demonstrate proper technique.
3. *Train at an appropriate facility.* You should not be allowed to exercise unless the weight training facility is well maintained, clean, and safe. In many instances, adult facilities are not appropriate for young athletes.

4. *Do only appropriate lifts.* Never perform single maximal lifts or sudden explosive movements. Performing these types of lifts can significantly increase the risk of injury.
5. *Practice proper breathing.* When lifting weights, it is important to exhale when exerting the greatest force and inhale when moving the weight into position for the active phase of the lift.
6. *Use a spotter.* Never train alone. You should use a spotter for any exercise in which you can lose control of the weight.
7. *Use collars.* Always use collars on barbells and dumbbells.
8. *Warm up.* Always take time to adequately warm up before starting to lift.
9. *Be aware.* Always be alert to what is going on around you in the weight room. Accidents happen when people are being careless.
10. *Employ proper technique.* Never perform an exercise or lift a particular weight if you cannot use the correct technique. Most serious injuries in weight training occur from poor technique.

Improper lifting technique

LIFTING TECHNIQUE

Each exercise described in this book has a proper technique. Before adding weight to the bar, each exercise should be properly executed with the proper technique. Most weight lifting injuries can be prevented if proper technique is used.

- Always keep the weight close to your body.
- Lift with your legs.
- Avoid twisting when lifting.
- Lift the weight smoothly.
- Allow for adequate rest between sets.
- Never lift more than you are safely able to.
- Always use proper breathing.

Improper lifting technique

SPOTTING TECHNIQUE

Every young athlete needs to learn to be a good spotter. As the spotter, it is your responsibility to assist your partner in performing the exercise in a safe and effective manner. The first point you need to learn is to always communicate with your partner. Before your partner begins an exercise, ask how many repetitions he or she intends to do and if this is a new amount of weight. As spotter, you should have a plan of attack in mind if the lifter fails to lift the weight. Always be alert and ready to grab the weight at any time. You must be strong enough to lift your partner's weight if he or she fails. Ideally, you and your partner should be matched based on size and strength. As the partner performs the lift, correct any problems with the technique. Encourage and motivate your partner when training.

Proper spotting technique

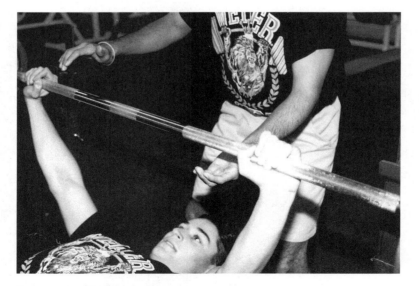
Proper spotting technique

WEIGHT TRAINING EXERCISES

CHEST EXERCISES
Bench Presses (Barbell)
Incline Bench Presses (Barbell)
Incline Bench Presses (Dumbbells)
Decline Bench Presses
Dumbbell Flyes

SHOULDER EXERCISES
Dumbbell Shoulder Presses
Dumbbell Lateral Raises
Dumbbell Front Raises
Medial Rotations
Lateral Rotations

ARM EXERCISES
Triceps Extensions
One-Arm French Curls
Dumbbell Kickbacks
Seated Dumbbell Curls
Preacher Curls
Concentration Curls
Wrist Curls

UPPER- AND LOWER-BACK EXERCISES
Upright Rows (Barbell)
Shoulder Shrugs
Lat Pull-Downs (Machine)
Back Extensions

LOWER-BODY EXERCISES
Barbell Squats
Lunges
Seated Calf Raises
Knee Extensions (Machine)
Hamstring Curls (Machine)

Chest Exercises
Bench Presses (Barbell)

Muscle Groups Worked: Pectoralis major (chest muscle), deltoid (front of upper-arm and shoulder area), triceps brachii (back of upper arm)

Starting Position: Lie on your back on the bench with a shoulder-width grip on the bar and feet flat on the floor. Completely extend your arms in preparation for the lowering of the weight.

Exercise Technique: Lower the barbell to the midchest area (with the elbows out to the side) and press back to the extended position. A wider grip focuses more on the pectorals, while a narrower grip focuses more on the triceps.

Safety and Spotting Techniques: Spotter: stand behind the lifter and lift the barbell off to him or her when ready. It is important that you pay attention at all times and follow the bar with your hands, as failure can occur suddenly in this or any other free-weight lift.

Bench Presses (Barbell)—
starting position

Bench Presses (Barbell)—
finishing position

Incline Bench Presses (Barbell)

Incline Bench Presses (Barbell)

Muscle Groups Worked: Pectoralis major (chest muscle), deltoid (front of upper-arm and shoulder area), triceps brachii (back of upper arm)

Starting Position: Lie back on a bench set at a 45-degree angle. Because of this angle, unlike the flat bench, a greater stress is placed on the upper-chest area. Once again have your feet on the ground and begin with the barbell in the arms-extended position in front of the face.

Exercise Technique: Lower the bar to the upper-chest area, near the clavicles, and then press the bar back to the extended position. Take care to press the bar up and back, in line with the supports, and not out and away from the body.

Safety and Spotting Techniques: Spotter: you are particularly useful here for lifting the bar off and replacing it again, given the nature of this exercise. Stand behind the lifter, either on the floor or on a small platform, and help to insure the lifter's safety.

Incline Bench Presses (Dumbbells)—
starting position

Incline Bench Presses (Dumbbells)—
finishing position

Incline Bench Presses (Dumbbells)

Muscle Groups Worked: Pectoralis major (chest muscle), deltoid (front of upper-arm and shoulder area), triceps brachii (back of upper arm)

Starting Position: Lie in exactly the same manner as in the barbell incline bench press, with the exception that you are using two dumbbells, held at shoulder height, palms facing outward.

Exercise Technique: Press the dumbbells up and back, focusing on pressing up evenly with both arms and keeping the back flat on the bench.

Safety and Spotting Techniques: Spotter: your position and duties are identical to those outlined in the barbell incline bench press. The only difference is that if you are needed, lift up under the lifter's elbows (and not on the bar as in the previous exercise).

Decline Bench Presses

Muscle Groups Worked: Pectoralis major (chest muscle), deltoid (front of upper-arm and shoulder area), triceps brachii (back of upper arm)

Starting Position: Lie on the decline bench with your ankles hooked under the pads and the midline of the chest directly under the bar. Grip spacing choice is the same as with other bench exercises. Extend the arms and focus on the bar.

Exercise Technique: Lower the bar to the midline of the chest while focusing on keeping the elbows out to the side of the body.

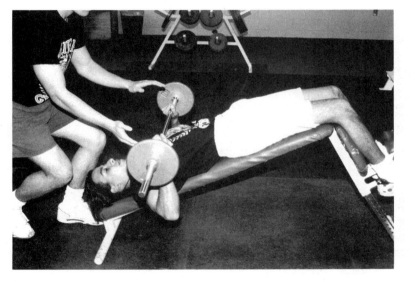

Decline Bench Presses—starting position

Decline Bench Presses—finishing position

Dumbbell Flyes

Muscle Groups Worked: Pectoralis major (chest muscle), deltoid (front of upper-arm and shoulder area), serratus anterior (side of upper-chest area)

Starting Position: Lie on either a flat or incline bench with the feet comfortably spread and braced for support. Hold a dumbbell in each hand with the arms out to the side (as far as you can safely go)

and bent at a 90-degree angle.

Exercise Technique: Bring the dumbbells together above the chest area while maintaining the arm angle previously described. Imagine hugging a tree or barrel while performing this technique. The spotter's job remains as described in the previous chest exercises.

Dumbbell Flyes—starting position

Dumbbell Flyes—finishing position

Dumbbell Shoulder Presses—starting position

Shoulder Exercises
Dumbbell Shoulder Presses

Muscle Groups Worked: Deltoid (front of upper-arm and shoulder area), triceps (back of upper arm)

Starting Position: Perform this exercise either standing or seated on a bench. In the standing press, start with the dumbbells in front of the shoulder area with the palms facing away from the body. This position is identical to that for the seated press, except that you are seated (and may receive more back support if you are using an upright bench).

Exercise Technique: Push the dumbbells upward until the arms are extended.

Safety and Spotting Techniques: Lifter: take care to avoid any arching of the back during this movement. Correct form would also include pushing up both dumbbells at an even pace.

Dumbbell Shoulder Presses—finishing position

Spotter: Stand behind the lifter and assist by lifting up on the elbows if the lifter needs help.

Dumbbell Lateral Raises

Muscle Groups Worked: Deltoid (front of upper-arm and shoulder area—primarily the lateral head)

Starting Position: Stand with the dumbbells held alongside the body with the palms turned inward (toward the hip).

Exercise Technique: Lift the dumbbells to a position where the arms are parallel with the floor. As much as possible, avoid using other muscles to assist in this and other isolation exercises.

Dumbbell Lateral Raises—starting position

Dumbbell Lateral Raises—finishing position

Dumbbell Front Raises

Muscle Groups Worked: Deltoid (front of upper-arm and shoulder area—primarily the anterior head)

Starting Position: Once again, stand with one arm holding the dumbbell (palm facing the body) forward of the thigh area. Brace the body on the hip area with the other arm.

Exercise Technique: Lift the dumbbell away from the body until the arm reaches a position parallel to the floor.

Dumbbell Front Raises—starting position

Dumbbell Front Raises—finishing position

Medial Rotations

Muscle Groups Worked: Subscapularis (one of four rotator cuff muscles)
Starting Position: Lie on your back on the mat with the dumbbell held in the palm, which faces the torso. Keep arm at a 90-degree angle and in contact with the mat.
Exercise Technique: Rotate the arm inward until the lower arm is vertical to the floor. Keep the elbow stationary.

Medial Rotations—starting position

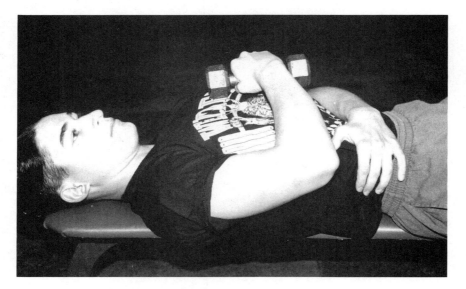

Medial Rotations—finishing position

Lateral Rotations

Muscle Groups Worked: Infraspinatus and teres minor (two of four rotator cuff muscles)

Starting Position: Lie on your side on the mat with the dumbbell held in front of the torso (palm facing the body). Bend your arm at a 90-degree angle with the upper arm resting on the torso.

Exercise Technique: Rotate the arm away from the floor to a point where it is vertical to the ceiling. Keep the elbow motionless throughout.

Lateral Rotations

Arm Exercises
Triceps Extensions

Muscle Groups Worked: Triceps and anconeus (back of upper arm)

Starting Position: Start by lying on your back on a bench with the feet up on the bench or on the floor. Raise the elbows and keep them in close to the body while holding the weight above the forehead or behind the head. The grip is palms away and shoulder width or slightly narrower.

Exercise Technique: At this point (while keeping the elbows together), push the weight away from the head until you reach the extended position. Do not jerk or hyperextend the arm at the end of the movement.

Safety and Spotting Techniques: Spotter: assist the lifter by standing behind and holding the elbows in during the movement. In addition, help the lifter when he or she is fatigued, and prevent the bar from being dropped on the head. Remind the lifter that he or she should never sit upright with the weight but should roll it down the torso or hand it to you.

Triceps Extensions— starting position

Triceps Extensions— finishing position

One-Arm French Curls—starting position

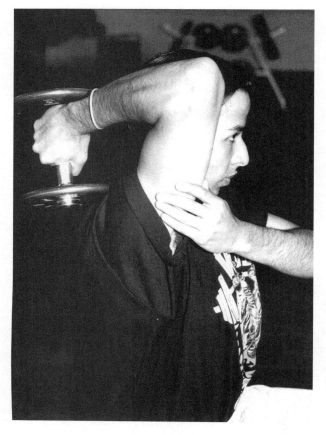

One-Arm French Curls—finishing position

One-Arm French Curls

Muscle Groups Worked: Triceps and anconeus (back of upper arm)
Starting Position: You may be standing or seated with the back straight and a dumbbell grasped in one hand (palm facing the head). Raise the arm vertically with the elbow bent and the weight held behind the deltoid area. Support the arm holding the weight at the elbow with the opposite arm.

Exercise Technique: Extend the arm toward the ceiling, raising the weight to the upright position. Keep the elbow (and the rest of the body) motionless.

Dumbbell Kickbacks

Muscle Groups Worked: Triceps and anconeus (back of upper arm)

Starting Position: You may do this exercise standing or bracing on a bench. If you are standing, brace the opposite arm on the opposite knee, with the back inclined slightly, but straight. Bend the arm with the dumbbell at a 90-degree angle with the elbow held up and close to the body while the weight is forward of the thigh.

Exercise Technique: Extend the arm away from the body until the weight reaches a point where it is parallel to the floor. Keep the elbow high and motionless throughout.

Dumbbell Kickbacks—starting position

Dumbbell Kickbacks—finishing position

Seated Dumbbell Curls

Muscle Groups Worked: Biceps brachii and brachioradialis (front of upper arm)
Starting Position: Sit on the bench holding the dumbbells with the palms facing away from the body.
Exercise Technique: Curl the dumbbells up to the torso, either one at a time or simultaneously. It is important to keep the elbows alongside the torso throughout and to make certain that the weights are lifted and not thrown.

Seated Dumbbell Curls—starting position

Seated Dumbbell Curls—finishing position

Preacher Curls

Muscle Groups Worked: Biceps and brachioradialis (front of upper arm)
Starting Position: Stand behind an incline bench (usually at a 45-degree angle) or sit behind a preacher curl station. Spread the legs for stability. The arms are in the extended position on the bench, holding the barbell with the palms facing upward.
Exercise Technique: Curl the barbell toward the torso without involving the assistance of any other muscles. Always train both sides in this or any other single-limb movement.

Preacher Curls—starting position

Preacher Curls—finishing position

Concentration Curls

Muscle Groups Worked: Biceps and brachioradialis (front of upper arm)
Starting Position: Sit on the side of a bench with the feet spread. Make sure that the arm holding the dumbbell has the palm upward toward the face. Extend the arm with the dumbbell close to the floor.
Exercise Technique: Curl the arm, bringing the dumbbell up to the torso. Keep the elbow static.

Concentration Curls—starting position

Concentration Curls—finishing position

Wrist Curls—flexion

Wrist Curls—extension

Wrist Curls

Muscle Groups Worked: Flexor carpi radialis and flexor carpi ulnaris (palm side of forearm)

Starting Position: Sit or kneel with the forearms supported on the bench or your legs (hands hanging over the edge). The palms of the hands are facing upward and holding the barbell.

Exercise Technique: Curl the palms toward the forearm until you reach the limit of the range of motion. Keep the arms in contact with the support throughout.

Upper- and Lower-Back Exercises
Upright Rows (Barbell)

Muscle Groups Worked: Trapezius (largest muscle of upper-back and neck area), deltoid (front of upper-arm and shoulder area)

Starting Position: Stand erect with the feet together, and hold the barbell with the hands about six inches to a foot apart (palms facing the torso).

Exercise Technique: Pull the barbell up to either the collarbone or chin level. It is important that you concentrate on keeping the back straight and the elbows out to the side while lifting.

Upright Rows (Barbell)—starting position

Upright Rows (Barbell)—finishing position

Shoulder Shrugs

Muscle Groups Worked: Trapezius (largest muscle of upper-back and neck area)
Starting Position: Stand erect with the arms hanging (palm toward the torso) holding the barbell.

Exercise Technique: Keep the arms extended as the shoulders are elevated or shrugged to as high a position as is feasible. Keep the rest of the body motionless and stabilized.

Shoulder Shrugs--starting position

Shoulder Shrugs—finishing position

Lat Pull-Downs (Machine)—starting position

Lat Pull-Downs (Machine)—finishing position

Lat Pull-Downs (Machine)

Muscle Groups Worked: Latissimus dorsi (major back muscle—middle and lower back)

Starting Position: Sit with the legs under the pads on the lat pull-down machine. The pads should fit closely, but they should not cramp you. Extend the arms overhead (palms away) and grasp the pulldown bar. A wider grip on this machine will work a more narrow range of motion, while a shoulder-width grip will work the muscle through a greater range of motion.

Exercise Technique: Pull the bar down to the upper-chest area while leaning back slightly (but still keeping the back straight). Another variation is to bring the bar down behind the neck to touch on the shoulder area. In either case, focus on driving the elbows down and avoiding dangerous bouncing or swaying of the body while performing this exercise.

Back Extensions

Muscle Groups Worked: Erector spinae group (originates in lower back and covers an area up to the seventh cervical vertebra)

Starting Position: Lie face down with the upper part of the hip area on the edge of the back-raise bench. The heels are held firmly by a spotter. Keep both the legs and back (which is above the floor) straight. Cross the hands over the chest or behind the head.

Exercise Technique: Lower the upper body. Then return from this position to the upright phase, where the body is parallel to the floor. Take care not to exceed this point, thereby hyperextending the back and increasing the risk of an injury to this area.

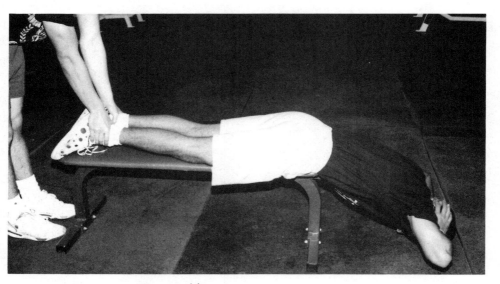

Back Extensions—starting position

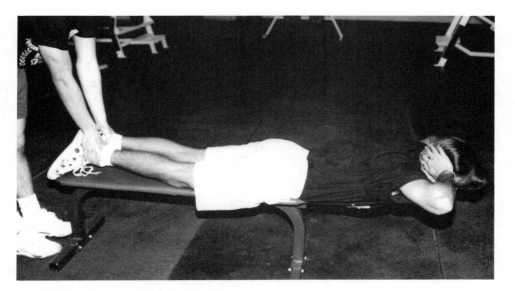

Back Extensions—finishing position

Lower-Body Exercises
Barbell Squats

Muscle Groups Worked: Gluteus maximus (butt muscle), quadriceps group (front of thigh), hamstring group (back of thigh), erector spinae (low-back area), gastrocnemius and soleus (calf muscle)
Starting Position: Get "under" the bar (which is in a squat rack or stand), placing it across your upper-back area on the

Barbell Squats

trapezius muscle. A shoulder-width or wider, depending on comfort, grip is taken on the bar. Before squatting down, have the proper mind-set. Focus on keeping your back straight, looking forward throughout the movement, and staying balanced (not swaying forward or backward).
Exercise Technique: Once ready, lower yourself in control to the bottom position. This position can be as high as a 90 degree knee angle or as low as having the thighs parallel to the floor. The depth of position is determined by how low you can go and still keep correct form (no lower) and by your goals (a lower position works the gluteus maximus and hamstring group more effectively). Then push out of the bottom position with control and good form. Don't rush this exercise—particularly the descent phase. Knees and backs can be hurt if done incorrectly!
Safety and Spotting Techniques: Always perform this exercise with a spotter (who stands behind the lifter and lifts up on the waist as needed) and a good belt (cinched tight enough to give support). In addition, it is important that you always perform this exercise in an area designed for squats—at a rack or squat stand. If these cautions are observed, squats will become one of your most productive and enjoyable exercises.

Lunges

Muscle Groups Worked: Gluteus maximus (butt muscle), quadriceps group (front of thigh), hamstring group (back of thigh)
Starting Position: This exercise can be done with either a barbell or dumbbells. If done with a barbell, have the barbell across the shoulders with the arms supporting it. When using dumbbells, hold them at the side (palms facing inward) throughout. Either way, the technique for the back and legs is the same. Stand erect with the legs assuming a shoulder-width stance.
Exercise Technique: Step forward with either leg (you may alternate legs or do one leg at a time) and descend until a 90-degree angle is reached by the lead knee. Keep the back straight and look forward, not downward. Take care to keep the knee directly over the foot, in a vertical line. From this point, push yourself up and back to resume the starting position.

Lunges

Seated Calf Raises—starting position

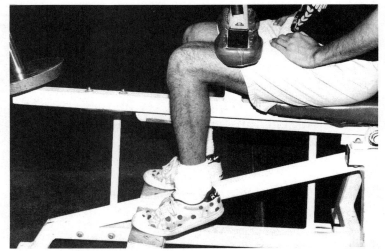

Seated Calf Raises—finishing position

Seated Calf Raises

Muscle Groups Worked: Gastrocnemius and soleus (calf muscle)

Starting Position: This exercise can be performed with a machine or with free weights. If you have a machine available, sit on the seat and place the pads on the thigh, about three to six inches behind the knee joint. Roll the ball of the foot on the platform with the heels below the platform. If no machine is available, you may simply place a barbell on the thighs (in the position described earlier) on top of a towel for comfort. Place the feet on a block of wood anywhere from four to six inches thick.

Exercise Technique: Raise up on the ball of the foot, elevating the heel as far as possible. Then lower the heel until you can take it no lower.

Safety and Spotting Techniques: When using the seated calf raise machine, do not go to failure (the point of exhaustion where you can't finish the exercise with the correct technique) as it will be difficult to get the safety bar under the movement arm if you cannot lift the weight high enough. When using free weights, either have a spotter remove the bar when you're done or stand the bar on one end to get up.

Knee Extensions (Machine)

Muscle Groups Worked: Quadriceps group (front of thigh)

Starting Position: Sit upright on the leg extension station. You should be positioned so that your knees are even with the axis of rotation on the machine (the joint around which the movement arm rotates) and so that the pads contact your lower-shin/ankle area. Bend the legs at a 90-degree angle and keep the lower leg perpendicular to the floor. Brace yourself by holding onto the side of the bench (in some cases handles are provided).

Exercise Technique: Extend your lower leg until it reaches a point parallel to the floor but stopping short of hyperextension. Focus on only using the quadriceps muscles and not jerking or throwing the weight with cheating motions which risk injury.

Knee Extensions (Machine)—starting position

Knee Extensions (Machine)—finishing position

Hamstring Curls (Machine)

Muscle Groups Worked: Hamstring group (muscles in the back of the upper leg)

Starting Position: Lie face down on the leg curl bench with the knees just past the edge of the bench (even with the axis of rotation on the machine). The pads contact your legs just below the base of the calf muscle, and the toes are pointed toward the floor.

Exercise Technique: Pull the lower leg toward the upper leg until a 90-degree knee angle is achieved. It is important that you try to prevent any excessive arching of the low back or lifting of the hips off the bench. Some benches are angled to aid in preventing these problems.

Hamstring Curls (Machine)—starting position

Hamstring Curls (Machine)—finishing position

Part III
Nutrition and Ergogenic Aids

9   Nutrition for the Young Athlete

Good nutrition habits will help you develop strength and improve your athletic abilities. What you eat every day affects how you grow and develop, how much energy you have, and how well you are able to train. When you eat, you provide fuel for your body. Think of your body as a car; if you put cheap gas in it and don't tune it up once in a while, it runs poorly and will eventually break down. Similarly, if you don't eat a balanced diet your body will not be able to perform at an optimal level. Most medical experts agree that the majority of chronic diseases such as cancer, diabetes, obesity, and heart disease are directly linked to poor nutrition. Today's successful athletes are nutrition wise!

There are approximately 50 nutrients in food that are believed to be essential for the body's growth, maintenance, and repair. These are classified into six categories: carbohydrates, fats, proteins, vitamins, minerals, and water. The first three provide energy, which is measured in calories. The latter are important for normal bodily functions. Today, athletes are learning how to eat right and eat smart.

BASIC NUTRITION PRINCIPLES

The three basic foods, carbohydrates, fats, and proteins, provide the energy for every function of the human body. A good diet is composed of 55 percent to 60 percent carbohydrates, 25 percent to 30 percent fat, and 10 percent to 15 percent protein. For athletes, experts often recommend 70 percent to 80 percent complex carbohydrates, 10 percent to 15 percent fat, and 15 percent to 20 percent protein. The best way to eat a balanced diet is to eat a variety of foods. The Food Guide Pyramid, discussed later, will help you make the right nutritional choices so that you can meet your nutrient needs.

Carbohydrates

Carbohydrates are often referred to as the primary supply of fuel for strenuous physical activity. They are found almost exclusively in plant sources and are classified as simple or complex. Examples of simple carbohydrates include table sugar, glucose, honey, and molasses. Examples of complex carbohydrates include grains, beans, potatoes, vegetables, and rice. Starches such as rice, potatoes, cereal, grains, and vegetables supply energy, vitamins, minerals, fiber, and water. A healthy diet should be high in complex carbohydrates and low in simple carbohydrates. At least 50 to 60 percent of an athlete's diet should come from complex carbohydrates.

During digestion and metabolism, carbohydrates are broken down and converted to glucose (simple sugars), the basic structural unit of all carbohydrates and the body's primary energy source. Some glucose is not needed right away and is stored as glycogen in the liver and muscle cells. Glycogen can be broken down into glucose and released into the bloodstream when needed. The body can store glycogen only in limited amounts. Thus, athletes strive to minimize glycogen depletion during training and competition. When glycogen stores become severely depleted, athletes begin to experience extreme fatigue, a phenomenon referred to as "hitting the wall."

Athletes should avoid high intakes of simple sugars. It was once believed that consuming some honey, table sugar, or candy immediately before an athletic competition would provide an immediate source of energy and improve performance. But it appears that just the opposite happens. Research has shown that snacks high in simple sugar cause a rapid increase in blood glucose, followed by a rapid decrease, with

COMPARISON OF COMMON FOODS WITH AN EQUIVALENT SUBSTITUTE HAVING A LOWER GLYCEMIC RESPONSE				
Eat less of these		Eat more of these	
FOOD	GLYCEMIC RESPONSE	FOOD	GLYCEMIC RESPONSE
Sugars			
Glucose	100	Fructose	20
Honey	87		
Vegetables			
Parsnips	98	Soybeans	15
Carrots	90	Kidney	
White	70	beans	30
potatoes		Lentils	25
		Sweet	
		potatoes	48
Fruit			
Bananas	65	Apples	36
Raisins	68	Oranges	40
Dates	72		
Grains			
White		Whole	
flour		wheat	
spaghetti	56	spaghetti	40
Cornflakes	85	Oats	48
White		Brown	
rice	70	rice	60
White		Buckwheat	
flour		pancakes	45
pancakes	66	Whole	
White		wheat	
bread	76	bread	64

Source: Michael Colgan, Ph.D. "Effects of Multi-Nutrient Supplementation on Athletic Performance." *I.F.B.B. Special Report.* International Federation of Bodybuilders.

a resulting increase in the rate of glycogen loss. Not all simple sugars cause such drastic fluctuation in blood glucose. By using the table above, athletes can choose foods that provide high energy but do not cause a rapid rise in blood glucose. The glycemic response of a food indicates how long it takes blood sugar to respond to ingestion of certain foods. The slower the response, the better.

Carbohydrates are important for all athletes regardless of the sport. Runners and bodybuilders alike need this fuel for performing their desired type of exercise. It is important to remember that carbohydrates are not fattening. They supply only four calories per gram consumed, as compared to fats which offer nine calories per gram. Carbohydrates are only fattening when they are consumed with other fattening foods. Remember, carbohydrates are the staple of any successful athlete's diet.

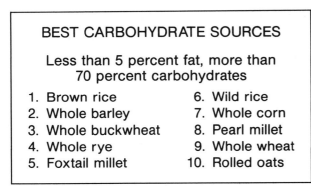

BEST CARBOHYDRATE SOURCES

Less than 5 percent fat, more than 70 percent carbohydrates

1. Brown rice
2. Whole barley
3. Whole buckwheat
4. Whole rye
5. Foxtail millet
6. Wild rice
7. Whole corn
8. Pearl millet
9. Whole wheat
10. Rolled oats

Source: Michael Colgan, Ph.D. "Effects of Multi-Nutrient Supplementation on Athletic Performance." *I.F.B.B. Special Report.* International Federation of Bodybuilders.

Proteins

Athletes have been consuming large quantities of protein for centuries, believing that eating lots of steak will build extra muscle. However, excess protein consumption does not build muscles; exercise builds muscles. Lifting weights builds muscles. Protein enhances muscle development, but it does not stimulate muscle growth by itself. If an athlete wants to bulk up, he or she needs to be involved in a comprehensive strength and weight training program and eat nutritious meals.

Proteins are often referred to as the building blocks of the body. They make up approximately 18 to 20 percent of the human body. The main function of protein is growth and repair. It is the structural basis for all body tissues. Protein can also be used for energy in some cases. Most athletes involved in strenuous training programs need to consume more protein than the average person. Although the National Academy of Sciences Committee on Recommended Daily Allowance (RDA) states that the daily protein requirement for active healthy adults is approximately 0.8 grams per kilogram of body weight, this amount is generally not enough for athletes. The RDA does not make allowances for heavy exercise, protein lost in sweat, and protein lost in the repeated minor injuries and inflammatory processes that are all part of an athlete's life.

Certain athletes, and especially growing athletes involved in strenuous resistance training programs and athletes recovering from injury, can consume up to 1.5 to 2.0 grams of protein per kilogram of body weight per day. Protein is required in proportion to the muscles' demand for increased tissue growth and repair. Thus, an athlete's protein requirement will depend on the sport, training program, injury status, weight, training goals, and time of the year (pre-, during, or postcompetition).

Growing athletes can consume 1.5 to 2.0 grams of protein per kilogram of body weight. (To convert your weight from pounds to kilograms, divide your weight by 2.2.)

Try to choose foods that are both high in protein and low in fat such as fish, chicken, turkey, lean meats, low-fat cheese, skim milk, and egg whites (see table at right).

BEST PROTEIN SOURCES

Less than 20 percent fat, more than 20 percent protein

1. Soybeans	6. Lima beans
2. Split peas	7. Black-eyed peas
3. Kidney beans	8. Lentils
4. Dried whole peas	9. Black beans
5. Wheatgerm	10. Navy beans

Source: Michael Colgan, Ph.D. "Effects of Multi-Nutrient Supplementation on Athletic Performance." *I.F.B.B. Special Report.* International Federation of Bodybuilders.

Fats

Fat is a very concentrated source of energy. Fats contain twice as many calories per gram (nine) as do carbohydrates (four). Fat is a secondary source of energy and is the primary storage form of foods not immediately utilized by the body. Fat deposits in the body are a fuel reserve. According to the American Heart Association, no more than 30 percent of a diet should consist of fatty foods. For athletes, 30 percent is too high. A high percentage of fat intake can result in decreased efficiency of the body and place added stress on the heart and joints. Furthermore, a high-fat diet leads to an increase in body fat, makes you feel tired, and impedes athletic performance.

In almost all cases, athletes, especially teenagers, should reduce their fat intake. Teenagers are notorious for eating too much fast food such as burgers, fries, donuts, ice cream, and milk shakes. High-fat diets contribute to heart disease, which, by the way, begins in childhood. Instead of donuts, try bagels; instead of eggs, try pancakes; instead of a hamburger, try pasta.

GRAMS OF PROTEIN AND CALORIES PER SERVING FOR BASIC FOODS

ONE SERVING	CALORIES
Milk—8 grams per serving	
1 cup skim milk	90
1 cup plain low-fat yogurt	90

ONE SERVING	CALORIES
Lean Meat—7 grams per serving	
1 ounce lean beef or pork	55
1 ounce chicken or turkey (no skin)	45
1 ounce fish, shrimp, lobster, or tuna	40
1 ounce low-fat cheese	55
2 large egg whites	35

ONE SERVING	CALORIES
Starchy vegetables, breads, and cereals—3 grams per serving	
½ cup cooked or dry cereal	80
½ cup cooked pasta	80
⅓ cup cooked rice	80
½ bagel	80
1 slice bread	80
1 small baked potato	80
¼ cup baked beans	80

ONE SERVING	CALORIES
Vegetables—2 grams per serving	
½ cup cooked vegetables	25
1 cup raw vegetables	25

ONE SERVING	CALORIES
Fruits—About 1 gram or less per serving	
1 small apple	60

Young athletes need to avoid eating a high-fat diet if they want to succeed in athletics.

Fat sources: (saturated) butter, cheese, chocolate, coconuts, oil, meats, milk, and poultry; (unsaturated) oil.

Vitamins

Vitamins are noncaloric organic substances essential for cell building, digestion, tissue building, and energy release.

Vitamins are present in small quantities in the body, and they promote many chemical reactions that occur naturally in the body. Recommended Daily Allowances (RDAs) have been established for most vitamins. However, remember that these are recommendations for the average daily amounts of nutrients that "a population" should consume. Some nutrition experts, such as Dr. Michael Colgan, feel that there is little use for the RDA when attempting to design nutrition programs for athletes. Although the ideal source of vitamins is a balanced diet, most adults, and certainly most teenagers, do not eat a balanced diet, and thus vitamin supplementation is recommended.

Most athletes need to consume high doses of vitamins to perform better. Because teenage athletes are not known for their nutritious diets, most need to take a daily multi-vitamin supplement to assure that all the important vitamins are being obtained.

Minerals

Minerals are inorganic substances that exist freely in nature. They are necessary for growth and repair of bones and teeth, metabolic activity, and function of body fluids and secretions. Minerals maintain or regulate such physiological processes as muscle contraction, normal heart rhythm, and nerve impulse conduction. For young athletes who are especially active and who sweat profusely for prolonged periods of time, it may be necessary to add additional salt and potassium to the diet. Both of these minerals can be easily replaced by drinking a sports drink, which can be purchased at any local grocery store. Consumers should read labels to make sure sports drinks are high in carbohydrates, are low in fat, and include sodium and potassium.

Mineral sources: the most essential minerals are calcium (found in milk, cheese, egg yolk, and green vegetables), iron (liver), iodine (seafood and iodized salt), and phosphorus (milk and cheese).

Iron

Most athletes, especially females and strict vegetarians, are deficient in iron. One sign of iron deficiency is excessive fatigue upon exertion. Iron is lost in sweat, through damage to red blood cells via "footstrike hemolysis," and in female athletes during menstruation. In addition, vegetarian athletes are also at risk for iron deficiency. Thus, females, vegetarians, and those athletes who eat little meat would benefit by taking an iron supplement.

Iron sources: orange juice, lean cuts of meat, enriched and fortified breads and cereals, and foods cooked in a cast iron skillet.

Water

Approximately 70 percent of the total body weight is water. Water is the most important nutrient, involved in almost every vital body process. Water is essential for maintaining the body's temperature, transporting materials, and assisting with chemical reactions. Two to three quarts of water should be ingested each day. Water level in the body is maintained by drinking fluids and by ingesting the water contained in fruits and vegetables. With excess sweating, such as during exercise and in hot humid weather, a large amount of water is lost. In such cases it is important to consume large quantities of water to remain hydrated.

- Exercise sessions should be reduced or curtailed when the relative humidity exceeds 90 percent and/or when the air temperature exceeds 85° F. Young athletes must be monitored carefully when exercising in the heat because they are more susceptible to heat-related illness than adults.

- The intensity of the exercise should be gradually increased over a 10- to 14-day period when moving to a warmer environment.
- Young athletes should always be fully hydrated prior to exercising in any type of environment (hot or cold). Athletes should be forced to drink during exercise, because at least one study has shown that children will voluntarily dehydrate themselves during exercise.

- These guidelines should be followed for ideal fluid replacement during exercise:

  1. The fluid should contain no more than 10–20 milliequivalents per liter of sodium and no more than 6 to 8 percent glucose or sucrose.
  2. The fluid should be cool (46° to 55° F).
  3. Fluids should never be restricted during exercise.
  4. For each pound of weight lost during exercise, two cups of fluid should be consumed before the next exercise session.
  5. Two and one-half cups of fluid should be consumed before practice or competition.
  6. At least one cup of fluid should be consumed every 15 to 20 minutes during exercise.

- In hot and humid environments, clothing should be lightweight to facilitate evaporation of sweat. In colder environments, layers of clothing provide an insulating barrier of air and can be

changed as the ambient temperature increases or decreases.

THE FOOD GUIDE PYRAMID

The Food Guide Pyramid, recently put out by the U.S. Department of Agriculture and the U.S. Department of Health and Human Services, is a new way to make the basics of a healthful diet easier to understand. It helps you make the right nutritional choices so that you can meet your nutrient needs by allowing you to select foods that together give you all the essential nutrients you need to maintain health without eating too many calories or too much fat.

The Food Guide Pyramid consists of five basic food groups (Levels 1–3) and the fats, oils, and sweets commonly found in our diet (Level 4). The size of the food-group piece corresponds to the recommended number of daily servings from that food group. For example, the bread-group piece is the largest in size, and it has the greatest number of recommended servings.

The triangle and circle shapes scattered throughout the Pyramid's pieces represent the added and naturally occurring fats and oils in certain foods, as well as the added sugars. Many triangles and/or circles in a food-group piece means that many of the foods in that category contain a large amount of naturally occurring or added fats, oils, and/or sugars. If you start at the bottom of the Pyramid and work your way up, you will see how selections from the food groups and other foods can be pieced together to form a healthful overall diet.

Level 1—Choose plenty of foods that come from grains. Whole wheat bread, cereal, rice, and pasta form the broad base of the Pyramid and should make up the bulk of your diet.

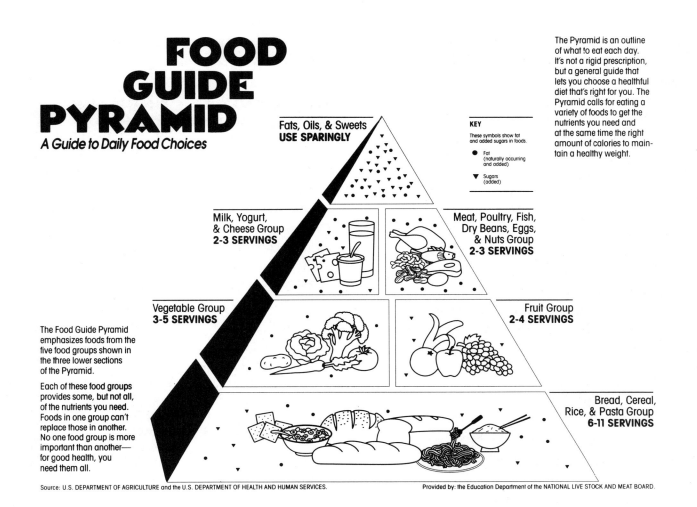

FOOD GUIDE PYRAMID
A Guide to Daily Food Choices

Fats, Oils, & Sweets
USE SPARINGLY

KEY

These symbols show fat and added sugars in foods.

● Fat (naturally occurring and added)

▼ Sugars (added)

The Pyramid is an outline of what to eat each day. It's not a rigid prescription, but a general guide that lets you choose a healthful diet that's right for you. The Pyramid calls for eating a variety of foods to get the nutrients you need and at the same time the right amount of calories to maintain a healthy weight.

Milk, Yogurt, & Cheese Group
2-3 SERVINGS

Meat, Poultry, Fish, Dry Beans, Eggs, & Nuts Group
2-3 SERVINGS

Vegetable Group
3-5 SERVINGS

Fruit Group
2-4 SERVINGS

The Food Guide Pyramid emphasizes foods from the five food groups shown in the three lower sections of the Pyramid.

Each of these food groups provides some, but not all, of the nutrients you need. Foods in one group can't replace those in another. No one food group is more important than another— for good health, you need them all.

Bread, Cereal, Rice, & Pasta Group
6-11 SERVINGS

Source: U.S. DEPARTMENT OF AGRICULTURE and the U.S. DEPARTMENT OF HEALTH AND HUMAN SERVICES.

Provided by: the Education Department of the NATIONAL LIVE STOCK AND MEAT BOARD.

Level 2—Also important is an ample variety of fruits and vegetables. Fruits and vegetables are full of the vitamins, minerals, carbohydrates, and fiber you need to gain strength and stay healthy.

Level 3—Add a moderate amount of lower-fat and lean foods from the milk group and the meat group. Dairy products provide calcium that's important for a healthy skeleton. Foods from the meat group provide needed protein, iron, and zinc. When they are included in your diet as a side dish to cereals, grains, fruits, and vegetables, you'll make a big step toward strength gains and healthful eating.

Level 4—Go easy on your selection of foods containing fats, oils, and sweets. In moderation, these foods can fit into an athlete's diet. They should not, however, replace the nutrient-rich food choices found throughout Levels 1, 2, and 3.

For the average teenager, it is recommended that you eat the following number of servings per day:
Bread group—11
Vegetable group—5
Fruit group—4
Dairy group—2-3
Meat group—3

Examples of a Serving
WHOLE WHEAT BREAD, CEREAL, RICE, PASTA
1 slice of bread
½ bagel or hamburger bun
1 ounce of ready-to-eat cereal
½ cup of cooked cereal, rice, or pasta

VEGETABLES
1 cup of raw leafy vegetables
½ cup of other vegetables, cooked or chopped raw
¾ cup of vegetable juice

FRUITS
1 medium apple, banana, or orange
½ cup of chopped cooked or canned fruit
¾ cup of fruit juice

MILK, YOGURT, AND CHEESE
1 cup of milk or yogurt
1½ ounce of natural cheese
2 ounces of processed cheese

MEAT, POULTRY, FISH, DRY BEANS, EGGS, AND NUTS
2 to 3 ounces of cooked lean meat, poultry, or fish
½ cup of cooked dry beans, 1 egg, or 2 tablespoons of peanut butter = 1 ounce of lean meat

A Reminder
Remember to

- Eat a variety of lower-fat foods from among all the five groups (Levels 1–3) each day. No one food or food group can provide all the nutrients you need to develop a strong and healthy body.
- Make plant foods such as cereals, grains, vegetables, and fruits the basis of your diet.
- Eat moderate amounts of lower-fat foods from the milk group and the meat group.

- Go easy on fats, oils, and sweets (those naturally occurring as well as added).

NUTRITIONAL CONCERNS FOR GROWING BODIES

Adolescence is a period of rapid growth and development. During this period, individuals may gain 20 percent of their final adult height. Because of the rapid growth that accompanies this period of life, nutritional requirements must be increased. Some young athletes involved in high-intensity workouts may need to consume 3,000 to 4,000 calories or more per day to maintain weight.

DAILY DIETARY ENERGY REQUIREMENT FOR ADOLESCENTS

AGE	MEDIAN WEIGHT (KG)	DAILY ENERGY REQUIREMENT PER KG (CALORIES)	TOTAL CALORIES
Males			
10–12	34.5	63.8	2,201
12–14	44.0	54.5	2,398
14–16	55.5	47.7	2,647
16–18	64.0	44.5	2,848
Females			
10–12	36.0	54.2	1,951
12–14	46.5	45.2	2,101
14–16	52.0	41.3	2,147
16–18	54.0	39.8	2,145

NUTRITION AND ATHLETIC PERFORMANCE

Gaining Weight
Gaining weight for improved athletic performance is not an easy task. Obviously the young athlete wants to gain lean body mass (muscle) and not fat mass (body fat). Any program designed to help an athlete gain

weight must be accompanied by a strength training program. Each pound of increase in lean body mass requires approximately 3,000 to 3,500 calories of energy to support it. Adding 700 to 1,000 calories of food intake each day will support a gain of one to two pounds of lean body weight. To achieve this, try adding an extra snack, such as a bedtime peanut butter sandwich with a glass of milk. Eat larger-than-normal portions at meal time, such as two potatoes instead of one. Eat higher calorie foods, such as cranberry-raspberry juice instead of orange juice. Try a high-protein and carbohydrate, low-fat powdered or premixed drink. Young athletes may want to consult their family physician for more advice on gaining weight safely.

Losing Weight

Excess fat can limit an athlete's endurance and quickness. In sports such as wrestling and running, any excess fat will reduce the athlete's performance. Young athletes concerned about their desired body weight or level of body fat should have their percent body fat tested. This test is offered at most health clubs. If weight loss is indicated, weight loss should not exceed one to two pounds per week.

Gradual weight loss = 1 to 2 pounds per week for women and 2 to 3 pounds per week for men.

It is a good idea for athletes to keep food records. Try and become aware of what and how much you are eating on a daily basis. Athletes are often quite surprised at how much they eat after they write it down. Try and reorganize your meals so they are lower in fat and calories. Because young athletes have special nutritional requirements, it is best to have a physician plan a safe weight loss program. To assure that all vital nutrients are obtained daily, it is wise to take a vitamin and mineral supplement.

Achieving and Maintaining Competing Weight

Athletes have used just about every technique imaginable to "make the weight." A rapid decrease in weight is very unsafe, especially immediately before or during periods of high-intensity training. Rapid weight loss can affect muscle growth and development. Athletes and coaches should plan the training schedule based on an athlete's initial weight. Any weight loss/ gain plan should be carefully planned and should be centered around a balanced diet and sensible training. Remember, frequent weight fluctuations can significantly impair athletic performance.

Athletes should not rely on a single precompetition meal for an adequate diet; rather they should eat a carbohydrate-rich diet every day to enhance muscle glycogen storage.

The Precompetition Meal

What you eat before an athletic event will help determine how well you perform. A good precompetition meal helps to prevent hypoglycemia (abnormal decrease in blood sugar), decrease hunger feelings during competition, provide energy for the muscles, and provide adequate fluids for the body. Instead of the old standard pregame meal of steak, eggs, toast, and potatoes, today's pregame meal should include foods such as fruits, cooked vegetables, lean meats, and whole wheat bread. A pregame meal should be consumed no later than two and one-half hours before competition. Athletes are encouraged to not drastically change their diet on the day of competition.

High-Protein Diets

High-protein diets and protein supplements alone, without proper training, will not improve muscle growth and/or performance. Young athletes are encouraged to follow the recommendations listed on pages 129–130 regarding protein intake.

High-Carbohydrate Meals

A young athlete's diet should consist of high-energy, low-fat foods. Carbohydrates are the most important fuel for muscular work. As the intensity of your workouts increases, so should your carbohydrate intake. Carbohydrates are stored in the muscle as glycogen. When your muscles are sore and you feel fatigued, your glycogen stores have been depleted. Since glycogen is the principal carbohydrate used during exercise, athletes should eat a high carbohydrate meal before exercise to provide fuel for exercise and one after exercise to help replace the glycogen used up during exercise.

Sample High-Carbohydrate, High-Energy Meal

BREAKFAST
1 cup orange juice or ½ grapefruit
1 cup hot cereal
2 eggs
3 ounces of bacon, ham, or sausage
2 to 4 slices of whole wheat toast or
   hotcakes with butter
1 to 2 cups of hot chocolate

LUNCH
1 bowl of clam chowder
3 to 6 ounces of broiled fish
½ cup of cooked rice
Green salad with dressing
2 slices of bread
1 to 2 cups of milk

DINNER
1 bowl of cream of potato soup
2 pieces of broiled chicken
1 to 2 baked potatoes
1 to 2 pieces of cooked broccoli
¾ cup of strawberries
1 to 2 cups of milk

SNACKS
Fruits (especially dates, raisins, apples,
   and bananas)
Milk or a milkshake
Cookies

KEY POINTS

- Good nutrition is an important part of developing strength and improving your athletic abilities. What you eat every day affects how you grow and develop, how much energy you have, and how well you are able to train.
- The six categories of nutrients are carbohydrates, fats, protein, vitamins, minerals, and water. The first three provide energy, which is measured in calories. The latter are important for normal bodily functions.
- A good diet is composed of 60 percent to 70 percent carbohydrates, 15 percent to 20 percent fats, and 15 percent to 20 percent proteins.
- The main function of protein is growth and repair. It is the structural basis for all body tissues. The daily protein

requirement for active healthy adults is approximately 0.8 grams of protein per kilogram of body weight. Young athletes can consume up to 1.5 to 2.0 grams per kilogram of body weight per day.

- It is important that young athletes consume large quantities of water before, during, and following exercise.
- The Food Guide Pyramid makes the basics of a healthful diet easier to understand. It helps you to select foods that together give you all the essential nutrients you need to maintain health without eating too many calories or too much fat.

- A rapid decrease in weight is very unsafe, especially immediately before or during periods of high-intensity training. Frequent weight fluctuations can significantly impair athletic performance.
- A pregame meal should be consumed no later than two and one-half hours before competition. Athletes are encouraged not to drastically change their diet on the day of competition.
- A daily multivitamin supplement will help ensure that active growing athletes obtain all of the necessary vitamins and minerals they need.

Anabolic Steroids
and Other Ergogenic Aids

10

For some athletes, winning is everything! Some athletes are willing to risk their health and their life just to perform better. Many athletes, too many to mention, have been seriously injured and even killed as the result of taking illegal drugs to enhance their performance. The bottom line is, it's just not worth the risk. You don't need to take drugs to be a successful athlete. Taking legal or illegal drugs to enhance your performance will only hurt you in the long run. It will also hurt others in your life—your friends and your family.

> Winners don't need drugs to be the best they can be!
> Losers take drugs because they don't believe in themselves, their abilities, or their potential!
> Are you a winner or a loser?

ERGOGENIC AIDS

An ergogenic aid, simply defined, is any substance, process, or procedure which may, or is perceived to, enhance performance through improved strength, speed, response time, or endurance of the athlete. Athletes have been using various forms of ergogenic aids for years, probably dating back to the first Olympics. Ergogenic aids can be broken down into five classifications: nutritional aids, physiological aids, psychological aids, pharmacological aids, and mechanical and biomechanical aids.

1. Nutritional
   Amino acid supplements
   Carbohydrate loading
   Water

2. Physiological
   Blood doping
   Oxygen supplementation

3. Pharmacological
   Amphetamines
   Anabolic steroids
   Caffeine

4. Psychological
   Hypnosis
   Imagery
   Stress management

5. Mechanical/biomechanical
   Clothing
   Equipment

Some ergogenic aids are clearly safe and appropriate such as training methods, use of water, improved equipment, carbohydrate loading, warm-up techniques, mental-relaxation techniques, and cool-down techniques. Other ergogenic aids are clearly illegal and against all the principles of the spirit of competition. Such aids as anabolic steroids, amphetamines, and other agents are illegal and pose a health risk to the athlete. Another problem with ergogenic aids is that research is very conflicting regarding the effectiveness of certain ergogenic aids. Often an ergogenic aid will improve the performance of an athlete for no apparent reason, an effect referred to as a *placebo effect*.

Regardless of the lack of reliable research to prove the safety and effectiveness of certain ergogenic aids, athletes will continue to use them, and manufacturers will continue to develop new athletic aids. Coaches, parents, physical educators, and athletes need to become knowledgeable consumers. Don't believe everything you hear. Learn to be a smart athlete, not a foolish one.

> If it sounds too good to be true, it probably is!

DRUGS IN SPORTS

The world we live in is greatly impacted by both legal and illegal drugs. Legal drugs, when taken under a doctor's supervision, are usually good and help us to feel better and get well when we are ill. Illegal drugs, on the other hand, can result in damage to a person's health and ability to function. Both legal and illegal drugs can be abused and are no strangers to the world of sports. Athletes have been taking drugs to enhance performance dating back to the first Olympic Games. Drug use in sports continues to be a major problem.

There are a variety of reasons why athletes take drugs. Some take drugs to feel better, to do better, because others have told them to do so, and so on. However, there really is no good reason to risk your health, life, and career. No one wants to see a young athlete's career ruined from drugs. The only way to help prevent young athletes from experimenting with or abusing drugs is to educate them. This chapter discusses some of the common drugs used by strength and weight training athletes.

Anabolic Steroids

Anabolic steroids, when natural (e.g., testosterone), are formed in the testes and the adrenal glands. Essential steroid hormones make it easier for some cells to form additional protein. Remember from Chapter 9 that protein is essential to normal growth and development. Steroids increase the rates at which muscle gains and tissue repair occur.

Synthetic steroids were developed to treat certain forms of anemia and osteoporosis and for the prevention of muscle wasting in certain diseases. They are routinely prescribed to promote tissue growth in patients who have had to remain in bed

THE WINNING ATTITUDE

To develop the winning attitude you must:

Become excited, confident, and enthusiastic about your goals.

Give yourself permission to be a winner.

Winners have the ability to look inside themselves and find that special dream.

The winner always has a goal.

The winner stresses solutions, not problems.

Winners have plans to reach their goals.

Winners make total commitments to their goals.

Winners have positive attitudes in all elements of their lives. The more you think about, talk about, and write about a thing happening, the greater the certainty of that thing happening.

Winning is an inside job.

Self-discipline is the winners' creed.

Don't just achieve your goals, strive to exceed your goals.

Goals should identify minimum performance. They should never limit your performance.

Champions strive to exceed their limits:

By making the good better, and the better best.

They never let it rest until the good is better, and the better is best.

Real winners are champions in life, not just in sport.

Are you a CHAMPION?

—*United States Olympic Training Center*

---

for an extended period of time. Unfortunately, these synthetic steroids, which can only be prescribed by a physician, are now readily available on the black market and have found their way into locker rooms and gyms. It has been reported that 90 percent of male athletes in sports such as weight lifting, power lifting, and bodybuilding have used or will use steroids at some point in their career.

Anabolic steroids produce two major ef-

> Winners and champions alike do not use drugs, period!

fects on the body: androgenic and anabolic. *Androgenic* effects are responsible for the development of male secondary sex characteristics (facial hair, a deeper voice). *Ana-*

bolic changes include the growth and development of certain body tissues, such as the rapid increase in muscle during puberty. Athletes using synthetic steroids search for the right mix to maximize the anabolic effects and minimize the androgenic effects. Nevertheless, all anabolic steroids produce some androgenic effects.

Do steroids work? The answer is yes. Steroids have been shown to increase strength and muscle mass, but studies are inconsistent in their findings. Some studies have shown that equal amounts of strength and muscle mass gains can be achieved through high-intensity training and proper nutrition versus using steroids. So why do people keep taking something that has more risks involved than benefits? Unfortunately, most people who take steroids are unaware of the risks involved. Steroids are illegal and should not be taken without medical supervision. When you buy a drug off the street, you have no idea what is in it, where it was manufactured, or how it has been processed and handled. Can you imagine injecting something into your body when you have no idea what is in it or where or how it was produced?

> The bottom line is the potential benefits of taking steroids do not outweigh the potential risks. In addition, research has been inconsistent in demonstrating their effectiveness.

Major Side Effects and Health Risks of Anabolic Steroids

- Liver cancer
- Acne
- Baldness
- Increased body hair
- Increased nervousness
- Decreased testosterone production
- Increased risk of heart disease
- Leukemia
- Headaches
- Gastrointestinal problems
- High blood pressure
- Menstrual problems
- Breast enlargement (males)
- Breast shrinkage (females)
- Deeper voice (females)
- Prostate cancer
- Dizziness
- Nosebleeds
- Increased aggressiveness
- Increased urine production
- Water retention
- Oily skin
- Muscle cramps
- Kidney damage
- High cholesterol and triglycerides

- Young athletes who take steroids before reaching puberty risk causing a premature fusion of the growth plate in the bones, leading to stunted growth.

The American College of Sports Medicine, one of the most respected professional exercise and sports organizations, has published a position stand on anabolic-androgenic steroids based on a comprehensive literature review. Read its position statement in the box on the next page.

Growth Hormones

Growth hormones are hormones that help support growth and the development of body tissues. It has only been within the last 20 years that a safe synthetic hormone has been available. Synthetic hormones are often given to children to stimulate growth. Although athletes have been taking growth hormones in an effort to stimulate muscle growth, little research is available to substantiate the effectiveness of their use. Athletes often mix anabolic steroids with synthetic growth hormones to either enhance the overall effect of both drugs or to minimize the effect of one of the drugs. This procedure is referred to as *stacking*.

Amphetamines

An amphetamine is a synthetic structured drug similar to the naturally occurring chemical in our body called epinephrine. Like epinephrine, it produces stimulation of the central nervous system, resulting in increased alertness in motor and physical activity, decrease in fatigue, and sometimes insomnia. Once again, research has found conflicting evidence regarding the effect of amphetamines on performance. To date, no studies have conclusively demonstrated that taking amphetamines improves strength or athletic performance. Amphetamines are banned by the International Olympic Committee. Once again, the risks of taking amphetamines outweigh the potential benefits.

Major Side Effects and Health Risks of Amphetamines

- Affect the ability of the body to regulate temperature
- Increase blood pressure
- Cause insomnia
- Increase diuresis and body water losses
- Cause depression
- Increase heart irregularity
- Increase anxiety
- Increase basal metabolic rate, which leads to weight loss

NUTRITIONAL AIDS

Nutritional aids are the safest, most effective, and most readily available ergogenic aids. There are a variety of nutritional aids available. As Chapter 9 stated, proper nutrition is essential for optimal sports performance. Athletes should strive to get all of their necessary nutrients from eating a varied, balanced diet. However, because most teenagers are so active and have generally poor eating habits, a vitamin and mineral supplement will help assure they are getting essential daily nutrients. In addition, athletes who are trying to gain weight and those involved in high-intensity training may benefit from a liquid protein and carbohydrate drink.

Carbohydrates

Carbohydrates are the most important fuel for muscular work. Carbohydrates supply increased energy during periods of increased intensity of exercise. Athletes should avoid the intake of simple carbohydrates, such as honey and candy. These

---

1) The administration of anabolic-androgenic steroids to healthy humans below age 50 in medically approved therapeutic doses often does not of itself bring about any significant improvements in strength, aerobic endurance, lean body mass, or body weight.
2) There is no conclusive scientific evidence that extremely large doses of anabolic-androgenic steroids either aid or hinder athletic performance.
3) The prolonged use of oral anabolic-androgenic steroids has resulted in liver disorders in some persons. Some of these disorders are apparently reversible with the cessation of drug usage, but others are not.
4) The administration of anabolic-androgenic steroids to male humans may result in a decrease in testicular size and function and a decrease in sperm production. Although these effects appear to be reversible when small doses of steroids are used for short periods of time, the reversibility of the effects of large doses over extended periods of time is unclear.
5) Serious and continuing efforts should be made to educate male and female athletes, coaches, physical educators, physicians, trainers, and the general public regarding the inconsistent effects of anabolic-androgenic steroids on improvement of human physical performance and the potential dangers of taking certain forms of these substances, especially in large doses, for prolonged periods of time.

Copyright American College of Sports Medicine 1987: Position Stand, "The Use of Anabolic-Androgenic Steroids in Sports" Med. Sci. Sports Exerc. 19:5, pp. 534–539, 1987.

types of carbohydrates enter the blood system very rapidly and cause a rise in blood sugar and insulin secretion, which causes the blood sugar level to fall below normal values and reduces, rather than enhances, performance.

Carbohydrate loading is a method of enhancing the storage of muscle glycogen and increasing one's capacity for intense work. A good way of knowing if you have been successful at carbohydrate loading is to weigh yourself during the carbohydrate-loading period. Because glycogen binds to water, you will probably gain several pounds during carbohydrate loading. If you want to consume carbohydrates before or during exercise, try some of the commercially available sport drinks. You should try to pick a drink that contains 5 percent glucose and has sodium and potassium in it. Following competition, load up on your carbohydrates again. During an intense athletic event, your glycogen stores get depleted, and if you don't replace them soon after, you will continue to be very fatigued for several days following competition.

Carbohydrate-Loading Plan
Day 1—moderately long exercise bout, but not to exhaustion
Day 2—mixed diet, moderate carbohydrate intake, decreased exercise
Day 3—mixed diet, moderate carbohydrate intake, continued decrease in exercise
Day 4—mixed diet, moderate carbohydrate intake, continued decrease in exercise
Day 5—high-carbohydrate diet, moderate exercise
Day 6—high-carbohydrate diet, light exercise or rest
Day 7—high-carbohydrate diet, light exercise or rest
Day 8—competition

Amino Acid Supplements
Proteins are comprised of individual building blocks called amino acids. The quality of the protein is classified as complete or incomplete, depending on the type of amino acids and their percentage in the specific protein foods. There are nine essential amino acids that the body cannot manufacture. Complete proteins are those that contain all essential amino acids in the proper quantity. During the training and growing years, athletes should take a basic amino acid supplement. The egg white is the best standard of quality protein and contains the best ratio and quantity of essential amino acids. Incomplete proteins include grains, legumes, seeds, and nuts. A great morning or pre- or posttraining blender drink can be made quickly by mixing 1 to 2 cups low- or nonfat milk, egg whites from 2 eggs, liquid or powder protein supplement (optional), 1 to 3 teaspoons of brewer's yeast, and a little honey to sweeten the drink.

Liquid Meals (Predigested Liquid Meals)
Certain high-quality liquid meals combine all of the essential and nonessential amino acids in a quick, safe, and tasty way. These drinks can also help athletes gain lean weight during training. Liquid meals should contain all of the essential amino acids, and the majority of their calories should come from protein and carbohydrates. For more information on the safety and effectiveness of predigested meals, see the story by Joe Weider on the Mega Mass Study (pp. 150–154) in the January 1994 issue of *Muscle & Fitness*.

Vitamins and Minerals

If athletes plan with care, they can consume enough vitamins and minerals with a normal diet of 2,000 to 2,500 calories. However, most coaches insist that a daily vitamin and mineral supplement is good insurance for anyone. In addition, some athletes, especially female and strict vegetarian athletes, may need an iron supplement.

> Taking vitamin or mineral supplements above the minimum daily requirement does not increase physical performance.

Water and Electrolytes

Drinking plenty of fluids is essential for all athletes. Fluids transport nutrients to and from the working muscles, help dissipate heat, and eliminate waste products. Unfortunately, few athletes understand the importance of adequate hydration. It is important for athletes to drink plenty of fluids before, during, and after an athletic event. Drinking a fluid containing electrolytes and carbohydrates can enhance performance and improve recovery time.

KEY POINTS

- You don't need to take drugs to be a successful athlete. Taking legal or illegal drugs to enhance your performance will only hurt you in the long run. Taking drugs also hurts other people in your life, like your friends and your family.
- An ergogenic aid is any substance, process, or procedure which may, or is perceived to, enhance performance.
- There really is no good reason to take any kind of drug.
- Anabolic steroids make it easier for some cells to form additional protein. Steroid hormones increase the rate at which muscle gains and tissue repair occur.
- Synthetic steroids are very dangerous because of the lack of regulation in their production and distribution.
- Young athletes who take steroids before reaching puberty risk causing a premature fusion of the growth plate in the bones, leading to stunted growth.
- There is little substantial scientific evidence to suggest that growth hormones, amphetamines, vitamins, or amino acid supplements increase strength, power, or athletic performance.
- Carbohydrates are the most important fuel for muscular work.
- Drinking plenty of fluids is essential for all athletes, because fluids transport nutrients to and from the working muscles, help dissipate heat, and eliminate waste products.

Part IV
Sport-Specific Training

11   Sport-Specific Training Programs

This chapter contains 14 sport-specific strength and weight training routines. We have included calisthenic, tubing and manual resistant [(T) = tubing exercise; (M) = manual], and free-weight exercises. The resistance, sets, and repetitions for each set of exercises will vary depending on your initial level of conditioning and what part of the season you are in (before, during, or after competition). To determine the correct resistance, sets, and repetitions for you, follow the guidelines outlined in Chapter 2. In addition, ask your coach for recommendations on the proper selection of exercises and the correct resistance, sets, and repetitions for each exercise.

CONDITIONING FOR SOCCER

CALISTHENICS
Quadriceps Lifts
Pull-ups
Dips
Curl-Ups

TUBING AND MANUAL RESISTANCE
Squats (T)
Knee Flexions (M)
Lat Pull-Downs (T)
Upright Rows (T)
Biceps Curls (T)
French Curls (M)

FREE WEIGHTS
Squats
Knee Extensions (Machine)
Bench Presses (Barbell)
Dumbbell Shoulder Presses
Dumbbell Curls
Triceps Extensions

CONDITIONING FOR BASEBALL AND SOFTBALL

CALISTHENICS
Quadriceps Lifts
Gluteal and Hamstring Lifts
Back Lifts
Bench Dips
Twists
Hanging Knee Raises

TUBING AND MANUAL RESISTANCE
Squats (T)
Leg Curls (T)
Butterflyes (M)
Side Lateral Raises (M)
Curl-Ups (M)

FREE WEIGHTS
Knee Extensions (Machine)
Hamstring Curls (Machine)
Dumbbell Flyes
Medial Rotations
Lateral Rotations
Preacher Curls
Dumbbell Kickbacks

CONDITIONING FOR BASKETBALL

CALISTHENICS
Lunges
Calf Raises
Gluteal and Hamstring Lifts
Pull-Ups
Elevated Upper-Body Push-Ups
Supported Leg Raises

TUBING AND MANUAL RESISTANCE
Hip Flexions (M)
Knee Flexions (M)
Shoulder Presses (M)
One-Arm Press-Outs (T)
Side Lateral Raises (M)
Triceps Extensions (T)
Biceps Curls (T)
Leg Raises (M)

FREE WEIGHTS
Barbell Squats
Hamstring Curls (Machine)
Seated Calf Raises
Upright Rows (Barbell)
Dumbbell Shoulder Presses
Incline Bench Presses (Barbell)
One-Arm French Curls

CONDITIONING FOR TENNIS

CALISTHENICS
Lunges
Leg Adductions
Leg Abductions
Upright Dips
Pull-Ups
Twists
Curl-Ups
Hanging Knee Raises

TUBING AND MANUAL RESISTANCE
Squats (T)
Leg Curls (T)
Shoulder Presses (M)
Push-Ups (M)
Side Lateral Raises (M)
Lat Pull-Downs (T)
Upright Rows (T)
Curl-Ups (M)

FREE WEIGHTS
Lunges
Knee Extensions (Machine)
Shoulder Shrugs
Lat Pull-Downs (Machine)
Incline Bench Presses (Dumbbells)
Dumbbell Front Raises
Wrist Curls

CONDITIONING FOR ALPINE SKIING

CALISTHENICS
Lunges
Gluteal and Hamstring Lifts
Pull-Ups
Elevated Upper-Body Push-Ups
Supported Leg Raises
Twists
Hanging Knee Raises

TUBING AND MANUAL RESISTANCE
Knee Flexions (M)
Hip Flexions (M)
Leg Curls (T)
Lat Pull-Downs (T)
Shoulder Presses (M)
Ankle Plantarflexions (M)
Ankle Dorsiflexions (M)

FREE WEIGHTS
Lunges
Hamstring Curls (Machine)
Seated Calf Raises
Shoulder Shrugs
Upright Rows (Barbell)
Dumbbell Curls
Dumbbell Kickbacks

CONDITIONING FOR WRESTLING

CALISTHENICS
Lunges
Gluteal and Hamstring Lifts
Pull-Ups
Bench Dips
Push-Ups
Supported Leg Raises
Curl-Ups

TUBING AND MANUAL RESISTANCE
Squats (T)
Leg Curls (T)
Upright Rows (T)
Butterflyes (M)
Side Lateral Raises (M)
Biceps Curls (T)
One-Arm Press-Outs (T)

FREE WEIGHTS
Lunges
Knee Extensions (Machine)
Incline Bench Presses (Dumbbells)
Upright Rows (Dumbbells)
Seated Dumbbell Curls
Triceps Extensions

CONDITIONING FOR SWIMMING

CALISTHENICS
Quadriceps Lifts
Gluteal and Hamstring Lifts
Back Lifts
Pull-Ups
Dips
Hanging Knee Raises
Curl-Ups

TUBING AND MANUAL RESISTANCE
Hip Flexions (M)
Knee Flexions (M)
Lat Pull-Downs (T)
Upright Rows (T)
Butterflyes (M)
Side Lateral Raises (M)
Biceps Curls (T)
French Curls (M)
Curl-Ups (M)

FREE WEIGHTS
Barbell Squats
Knee Extensions (Machine)
Upright Rows (Barbell)
Bench Presses (Barbell)
Dumbbell Shoulder Presses
Dumbbell Curls
Triceps Extensions
Lunges

CONDITIONING FOR GYMNASTICS

CALISTHENICS
Lunges
Gluteal and Hamstring Lifts
Calf Raises
Pull-Ups
Elevated Upper-Body Push-Ups
Dips
Supported Leg Raises
Curl-Ups

TUBING AND MANUAL RESISTANCE
Squats (T)
Leg Curls (T)
Butterflyes (M)
Shoulder Presses (M)
Side Lateral Raises (M)
Ankle Plantarflexions (M)
Ankle Dorsiflexions (M)

FREE WEIGHTS
Lunges
Knee Extensions (Machine)
Seated Calf Raises
Upright Rows (Barbell)
Dumbbell Shoulder Presses
Incline Bench Presses (Dumbbells)
Dumbbell Lateral Raises
Seated Dumbbell Curls

CONDITIONING FOR VOLLEYBALL

CALISTHENICS
Gluteal and Hamstring Lifts
Calf Raises
Pull-Ups
Bench Dips
Curl-Ups

TUBING AND MANUAL RESISTANCE
Hip Flexions (M)
Knee Flexions (M)
Lat Pull-Downs (T)
Upright Rows (T)
Butterflyes (M)
Ankle Plantarflexions (M)
Curl-Ups

FREE WEIGHTS
Knee Extensions (Machine)
Hamstring Curls (Machine)
Incline Bench Presses (Dumbbells)
Seated Dumbbell Curls
Triceps Extensions
Seated Calf Raises

CONDITIONING FOR FOOTBALL

CALISTHENICS
Lunges
Pull-Ups
Dips
Twists
Back Lifts
Curl-Ups
Hanging Knee Raises

TUBING AND MANUAL RESISTANCE
Squats (T)
Lat Pull-Downs (T)
Upright Rows (T)
Shoulder Presses (M)
Side Lateral Raises (M)
Biceps Curls (T)
French Curls (M)
Leg Raises (M)

FREE WEIGHTS
Lunges
Hamstring Curls (Machine)
Upright Rows (Barbell)
Lat Pull-Downs (Machine)
Dumbbell Shoulder Presses
Incline Bench Presses
Dumbbell Front Raises
Knee Extensions (Machine)

CONDITIONING FOR RUNNING

CALISTHENICS
Gluteal and Hamstring Lifts
Pull-Ups
Push-Ups
Dips
Curl-Ups
Hanging Knee Raises

TUBING AND MANUAL RESISTANCE
Squats (T)
Knee Flexions (M)
Lat Pull-Downs (T)
Upright Rows (T)
Shoulder Presses (M)
Butterflyes (M)
Ankle Dorsiflexions (M)
Curl-Ups (M)

FREE WEIGHTS
Barbell Squats
Knee Extensions (Machine)
Upright Rows
Lat Pull-Downs (Machine)
Incline Bench Presses (Dumbbells)
Dumbbell Curls
One-Arm French Curls

CONDITIONING FOR CYCLING

CALISTHENICS
Gluteal and Hamstring Lifts
Pull-Ups
Back Lifts
Upright Dips
Bench Dips
Supported Leg Raises
Curl-Ups

TUBING AND MANUAL RESISTANCE
Squats (T)
Leg Curls (T)
One-Arm Rows (M)
Butterflyes (M)
Upright Rows (T)
Biceps Curls (T)

FREE WEIGHTS
Barbell Squats
Knee Extensions (Machine)
Bench Presses (Barbell)
Dumbbell Shoulder Presses
Triceps Extensions
Wrist Curls

CONDITIONING FOR TRACK (JUMPING EVENTS)

CALISTHENICS
Lunges
Gluteal and Hamstring Lifts
Calf Raises
Back Lifts
Upright Dips
Push-Ups
Supported Leg Raises
Curl-Ups

TUBING AND MANUAL RESISTANCE
Hip Flexions (M)
Knee Flexions (M)
Lat Pull-Downs (T)
Upright Rows (T)
Standing Chest Presses (T)
Ankle Dorsiflexions (M)
Ankle Plantarflexions (M)
Curl-Ups

FREE WEIGHTS
Lunges
Knee Extensions (Machine)
Seated Calf Raises
Lat Pull-Downs (Machine)
Incline Bench Presses (Dumbbells)
Dumbbell Shoulder Presses
Barbell Squats

CONDITIONING FOR GOLF

CALISTHENICS
Lunges
Gluteal and Hamstring Lifts
Calf Raises
Upright Dips
Push-Ups
Supported Leg Raises
Curl-Ups

TUBING AND MANUAL RESISTANCE
Hip Flexions (M)
Knee Flexions (M)
Lat Pull-Downs (T)
Upright Rows (T)
Standing Chest Presses (T)
Triceps Extensions (T)
Wrist Curls (T)
Biceps Curls (T)

FREE WEIGHTS
Lunges
Triceps Extensions
Lat Pull-Downs (Machine)
Incline Bench Presses (Dumbbells)
Dumbbell Shoulder Presses
Barbell Squats
Wrist Curls

Appendixes

Appendix A   Workout Chart

One of the most important rules of strength and weight training is to keep track of your progress. The best way to keep track of your progress is to keep a workout log—all great athletes keep detailed workout logs. You can make your own workout log using the workout log in Appendix A as a guide. Whichever workout log you create, it is important to include space to record the exercises performed each workout session, the number of sets and repetitions, and the resistance for each exercise, as well as any other comments you may want to note (e.g., this exercise is getting easier, increase the weight next time). When it comes time to make changes in your workouts, you should refer back to your workout charts. You can often identify problem areas in your program by looking back through your workout chart (e.g., your shoulders have been sore lately and you notice in your workout charts that you increased the resistance on your shoulder exercises twice that week and you also added two new shoulder exercises).

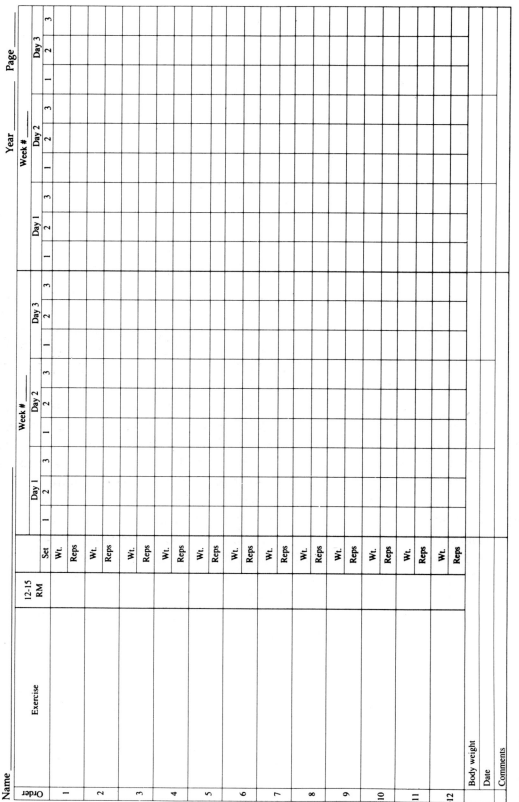

Name _____ Year _____ Page _____

Order | Exercise | 12-15 RM | Set | Week # | | | | | | | | | Week # | | | | | | | | |
|---|---|---|---|---|---|---|---|---|---|---|---|---|---|---|---|---|---|---|---|---|
| | | | | Day 1 | | | Day 2 | | | Day 3 | | | Day 1 | | | Day 2 | | | Day 3 | | |
| | | | | 1 | 2 | 3 | 1 | 2 | 3 | 1 | 2 | 3 | 1 | 2 | 3 | 1 | 2 | 3 | 1 | 2 | 3 |
| 1 | | | Wt. Reps | | | | | | | | | | | | | | | | | | |
| 2 | | | Wt. Reps | | | | | | | | | | | | | | | | | | |
| 3 | | | Wt. Reps | | | | | | | | | | | | | | | | | | |
| 4 | | | Wt. Reps | | | | | | | | | | | | | | | | | | |
| 5 | | | Wt. Reps | | | | | | | | | | | | | | | | | | |
| 6 | | | Wt. Reps | | | | | | | | | | | | | | | | | | |
| 7 | | | Wt. Reps | | | | | | | | | | | | | | | | | | |
| 8 | | | Wt. Reps | | | | | | | | | | | | | | | | | | |
| 9 | | | Wt. Reps | | | | | | | | | | | | | | | | | | |
| 10 | | | Wt. Reps | | | | | | | | | | | | | | | | | | |
| 11 | | | Wt. Reps | | | | | | | | | | | | | | | | | | |
| 12 | | | Wt. Reps | | | | | | | | | | | | | | | | | | |
| Body weight | | | | | | | | | | | | | | | | | | | | | |
| Date | | | | | | | | | | | | | | | | | | | | | |
| Comments | | | | | | | | | | | | | | | | | | | | | |

Workout Chart

Note. From Weight Training: Steps To Success (pp. 189–191) by T. R. Baechle and B. R. Groves, Champaign, IL: Leisure Press. Copyright 1992 by Leisure Press. Reprinted by permission.

Appendix B

The Human Muscular System

Appendix B provides a general overview of the human musculature system. It is important to learn the names and locations of the muscles of the body in order to perform weight-training exercises correctly. Each exercise described in this book lists the muscle(s) or muscle groups that are being worked for each particular exercise. A good way to begin learning the muscles of the body is to refer back to this Appendix each time you perform a particular exercise. Before you start an exercise, look at the muscle(s) or muscle groups being worked and then identify them on the illustrations in this Appendix. Soon you will be able to name exercises that develop a specific muscle(s) or muscle groups.

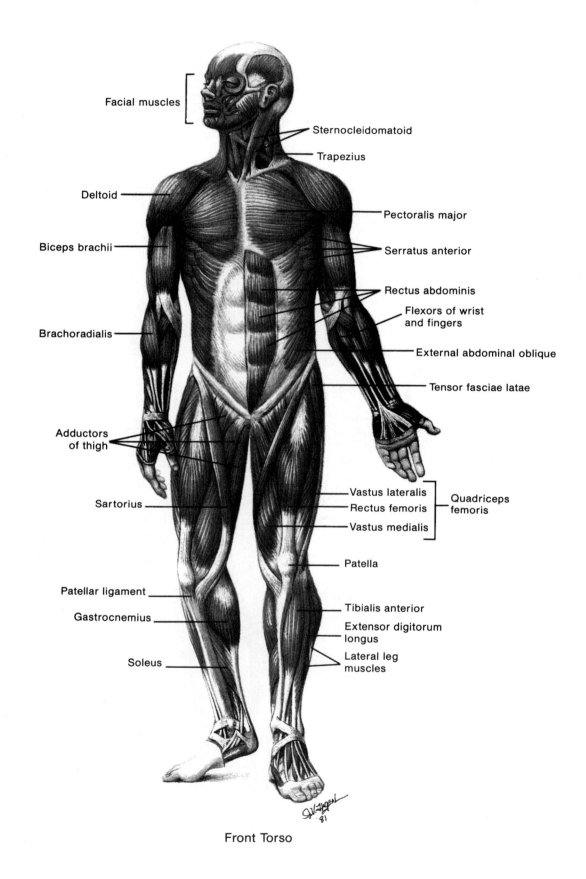

Facial muscles

Sternocleidomatoid

Trapezius

Deltoid

Pectoralis major

Biceps brachii

Serratus anterior

Rectus abdominis

Flexors of wrist and fingers

Brachoradialis

External abdominal oblique

Tensor fasciae latae

Adductors of thigh

Vastus lateralis

Rectus femoris

Quadriceps femoris

Sartorius

Vastus medialis

Patella

Patellar ligament

Tibialis anterior

Gastrocnemius

Extensor digitorum longus

Lateral leg muscles

Soleus

Front Torso

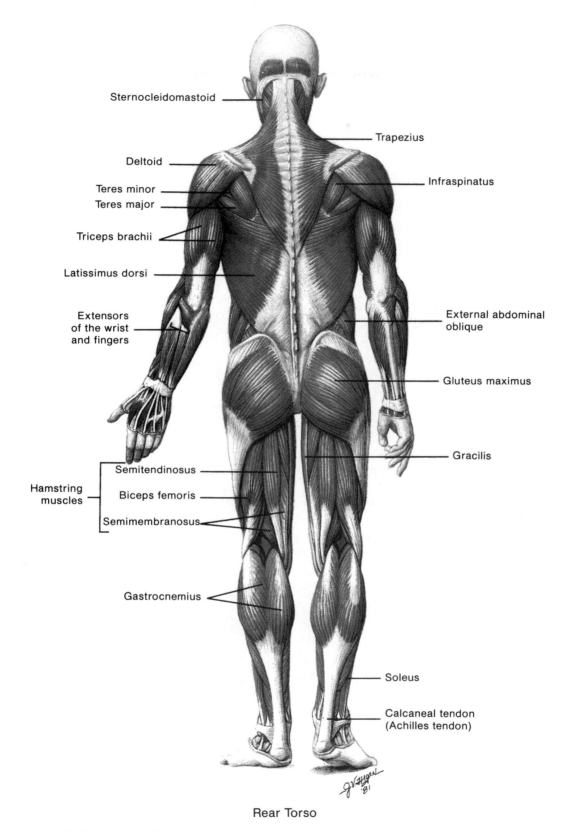

Sternocleidomastoid

Trapezius

Deltoid

Infraspinatus

Teres minor

Teres major

Triceps brachii

Latissimus dorsi

Extensors
of the wrist
and fingers

External abdominal
oblique

Gluteus maximus

Gracilis

Semitendinosus

Hamstring
muscles

Biceps femoris

Semimembranosus

Gastrocnemius

Soleus

Calcaneal tendon
(Achilles tendon)

Rear Torso

Source: R. Seeley, T. Stephens, and P. Tate,
Essentials of Anatomy and Physiology
(St. Louis: Mosby-Year Book, 1991), 158–159.

Appendix C

Strength and Weight Training Resources

American Academy of Pediatrics
141 Northwest Point Blvd.
P.O. Box 927
Elk Grove Village, IL 60009-0927

American College of Sports Medicine
P.O. Box 1440
Indianapolis, IN 46206-1440

American Orthopaedic Society for
  Sports Medicine
70 W. Hubbard St., Suite 202
Chicago, IL 60610

International Federation of
  Bodybuilders (IFBB)
2875 Bates Rd.
Montreal, Quebec, Canada H3S 1B7

National Strength and Conditioning
  Association (NSCA)
P.O. Box 81410
Lincoln, NE 68501

The National Youth Sports Foundation
10 Meredith Circle
Needham, MA 02192

Powerlifting U.S.A.
P.O. Box 467
Camarillo, CA 93011

United States Weightlifting
  Federation (USWF)
U.S. Olympic Complex
1750 E. Boulder St.
Colorado Springs, CO 80909

Appendix D

Strength and Weight Training Equipment

Weider, Inc., makes the world's finest strength and weight training equipment, as well as leading aerobics equipment. To order a catalog, contact:

Weider, Inc.
1500 South 1000 West
Logan, UT 84321
1-800-999-3102

Strength of America, Inc., was founded in 1989 with the goal of strengthening children's joints to help prevent injury and improve self-esteem in a safe and fun environment. Kids Power weight equipment was designed with safety as the primary concern. There are 11 stations that fit in less than 400 square feet of space and a computerized program to produce individualized workout cards. For more information on weight equipment and/or strength and conditioning programs for children, contact:

Strength of America, Inc.
P.O. Box 31447
Mesa, AZ 85275-1447
(602) 641-2417

Bibliography

American Academy of Pediatrics. 1982. "Climatic heat stress and the exercising child." *Pediatrics* 69 (6): 808.

American Academy of Pediatrics. 1983a. *Sports medicine: Health care for young athletes.* Evanston, IL: American Academy of Pediatrics.

American Academy of Pediatrics. 1983b. "Weight training and weightlifting: Information for the pediatrician." *The Physician and Sportsmedicine* 11:157–61.

American Academy of Pediatrics on Sports Medicine. 1983. "Weight training and weight lifting: Information for the pediatrician." *News and Comments* 33:7–8.

American Academy of Pediatrics on Sports Medicine. 1990. "Strength training, weight and power lifting, and body building by children and adolescents." *Pediatrics* 86 (5):801–2.

American College of Sports Medicine. 1987. "The use of anabolic-androgenic steroids in sports." *Medicine and Science in Sports and Exercise* 19:534–39.

American College of Sports Medicine. 1988. "Opinion statement on physical fitness in children and youth." *Medicine and Science in Sports and Exercise* 20:422–23.

American Orthopaedic Society for Sports Medicine. 1988. *Proceedings of the conference on strength training and the prepubescent.* Edited by B. Cahill. Chicago: American Orthopaedic Society for Sports Medicine.

Atha, J. 1981. "Strengthening muscle." In *Exercise and sport science reviews.* New York: Macmillan.

Baechle, T. R., and B. R. Groves. 1992. *Weight training: Steps to Success.* Champaign, IL: Leisure Press.

Bar-Or, O. 1980a. "Climate and the exercising child—a review." *International Journal of Sports Medicine* 1:53–65.

Bar-Or, O. 1980b. "Voluntary hypohydration in 10- to 12-year-old boys." *Journal of Applied Physiology* 48:104–8.

Bar-Or, O. 1983. *Pediatric sports medicine for the practitioner.* New York: Springer-Verlag.

Bar-Or, O. 1989. "Trainability of the prepubescent child." *The Physician and Sportsmedicine* 5:65–82.

Belko, A. Z. 1987. "Vitamins and exercise—an update." *Medicine and Science in Sports and Exercise* 19 (suppl.):191–96.

Blimkie, C. J. R., J. Ramsay, D. Sale, D. MacDougall, K. Smith, and S. Garner. 1989. "Effects of 10 weeks of resistance training on strength development in prepubertal boys." Edited by S. Oseid and K. H. Carlsen. In *International series on sport sciences. Children and exercise XIII.* Champaign, IL: Human Kinetics.

Brooks, G. A. 1987. "Amino acid and protein metabolism during exercise and recovery." *Medicine and Science in Sports and Exercise* 19 (suppl.): 150–56.

Brooks, G. A., and T. D. Fahey. 1984. *Exercise physiology: Human bioenergetics and its applications.* New York: Macmillan.

Buskirk, E. R. 1977. "Diet and athletic performance." *Postgraduate Medicine* 61:229–36.

Colgan, M. "Effects of Multi-Nutrient Supplementation on Athletic Performance." *I.F.B.B. special report.* International Federation of Bodybuilders.

Costill, D. 1979. "Adaptations in skeletal muscle following strength training." *Journal of Applied Physiology* 46:96–99.

Docherty, D., H. A. Wenger, and M. L. Collis. 1987. "The effects of resistance training on aerobic and anaerobic power in young boys." *Medicine and Science in Sports and Exercise* 19:389–92.

Ekbolm, B. 1969. "Effect of physical training in adolescent boys." *Journal of Applied Physiology* 27:350–55.

Gilliam, T. B. 1977. "Prevalence of coronary heart disease risk factors in active children, 7- to 12-years of age." *Medicine and Science in Sports and Exercise* 9:21–25.

Gortmaker, S. L. 1987. "Increasing pediatric obesity in the United States." *American Journal of Diseases of Children* 141:535-40.

Gumps, V. L., D. Segal, J. B. Halligan, and G. Lower. 1982. "Bilateral distal radius and ulnar fracture in weightlifting." *American Journal of Sports Medicine* 10:375–79.

Harkness, R. A., and B. H. Kilshaw. 1975. "Effects of large doses of anabolic steroids." *British Journal of Sports Medicine* 9:70–73.

Haskell, W., J. Scala, and J. Whittam, eds. 1982. *Nutrition and athletic performance.* Palo Alto, CA: Bull Publishing Co.

Komi, P. V. 1986. "Training of muscle strength and power: Interaction of neuromotoric, hypertrophic and mechanical factors." *International Journal of Sports Medicine* 7 (suppl.): 10–15.

Kraemer, W. J., A. C. Fry, P. N. Frykman, B. Conroy, and J. Hoffman. 1989. "Resistance training and youth." *Pediatric Exercise Science* 1:336–50.

Lamb, D. R. 1987. "Anabolic steroids in athletics: How well do they work and how dangerous are they?" *American Journal of Sports Medicine* 12:31–38.

Legwold, G. 1982. "Does lifting weights harm a prepubescent athlete?" *The Physician and Sportsmedicine* 10:141–44.

Metcalf, J. A., and S. O. Roberts. 1993. "Strength training and the immature athlete: An overview." *Pediatric Nursing* 19 (4):325–32.

Micheli, L. J. 1986. "Pediatric and adolescent sports injury: Recent trends." *Exercise and Sport Science Reviews* 14:359–74.

Micheli, L. J. 1988. "Strength training in the young athlete." Edited by E. W. Brown and C. F. Crystal. In *Competitive sports for children and youth: An overview of research and issues*. Champaign, IL: Human Kinetics.

Moritani, T., and H. DeVries. 1979. "Neural factors versus hypertrophy in the time course of muscle strength gain." *American Journal of Physical Medicine* 58:115–19.

Munson, W. W., and F. E. Pettigrew. 1988. "Cooperative strength training." *Journal of Physical Education, Recreation and Dance* (February): 61–66.

Nadel, E. R. 1988. "New ideas for rehydration during and after exercise in hot weather." *Sports Science Exchange* (Gatorade Sports Science Institute. Chicago.) 1 (3).

National Strength and Conditioning Association. 1985. "Position paper on prepubescent strength training." *National Strength and Conditioning Association Journal* 7:27–29.

Nielsen, B., K. Nielsen, M. Behrendt-Hansen, and A. Asmussen. 1980. "Training of function muscular strength in girls 7-19 years old." Edited by K. Berg and B. K. Erikson. In *Children and exercise*. Baltimore: University Park Press.

Pfeiffer, R. D., and R. S. Francis. 1986. "Effects of strength training on muscle development in prepubescent, pubescent, and postpubescent males." *The Physician and Sportsmedicine* 14 (9):134–43.

Ramsay, J. A., C. J. R. Blimkie, S. Smith, J. D. Garner, J. D. Macdougall, and D. G. Sale. 1990. "Strength training effects in prepubescent boys." *Medicine and Science in Sports and Exercise* 22(5): 605–14.

Roberts, S. O. 1993a. "Exercise trainability of children: Current theories and training considerations." In *Healthy from the start: New perspectives on childhood fitness*. Edited by M. Leppo. Washington, DC: ERIC Clearinghouse On Teacher Education.

Roberts, S. O. 1993b. "Protein overload." *Nautilus*. (January) 30–37.

Ross, J. G., and G. G. Gilbert. 1985. "National children and youth fitness study. A summary of findings." *Journal of Physical Education, Recreation and Dance* 56:45–50.

Rupnow, A. 1985. "Upper body strength: Helping kids win the battle." *Journal of Physical Education, Recreation and Dance* (October): 60–63.

Ryan, J. R., and G. G. Salciccioli. 1976. "Fracture of the distal radial epiphysis in adolescent weight lifters." *American Journal of Sports Medicine* 4:26–27.

Sale, D. G. 1988. "Neural adaptation to resistance training." *Medicine and Science in Sports and Exercise* 20:S135–45.

Sale, D. G. 1989. "Strength training in children." In *Perspectives in exercise science and sports medicine*. Edited by C. V. Gisolfi and D. R. Lamb. Carmel, IN: Benchmark Press.

Seeley, R., T. Stephens, and P. Tate. 1991. *Essentials of anatomy and physiology*. St. Louis: Mosby-Year Book.

Sevedio, F. J., R. L. Bartels, and R. L. Hamlin. 1985. "The effects of weight training, using Olympic style lifts, on various physiological variables in prepubescent boys (abstract)." *Medicine and Science in Sports and Exercise* 17:288.

Sewall, L., and L. J. Micheli. 1986. "Strength training for children." *Journal of Pediatric Orthopedics* 6:143–46.

Siegel, J. A., D. N. Camaione, and T. G. Manfredi. 1989. "The effects of upper body resistance training on prepubescent children." *Pediatric Exercise Science* 1:145–54.

Tanner, J. M. 1962. *Growth at adolescence*. Oxford, England: Blackwell Scientific.

Vrijens, J. 1978. "Muscle strength development in the pre- and post-pubescent age." *Medicine and Sport* 11: 157-61.

Weider, J. 1994. "Mega Mass Study." *Muscle & Fitness* (January): 150–54.

Weltman, A., C. Janney, C. Rians, K. Strand, B. Berg, S. Tippit, J. Wide, B. Cahill, and F. Katch. 1986. "The effects of hydraulic-resistance strength training in prepubertal boys." *Medicine and Science in Sports and Exercise* 18:629–38.

Weltman, A., C. Janney, C. Rians, K. Strand, and F. Katch. 1987. "Effects of hydraulic-resistance strength training on serum lipid levels in prepubertal boys." *American Journal of Diseases of Children* 141 (7): 777–80.

Wilkins, K. E. 1980. "The uniqueness of the young athlete: Musculoskeletal injuries." *American Journal of Sports Medicine* 8:377–82.

Williams, M. H. 1983. *Ergogenic aids in sport*. Champaign, IL: Human Kinetics.

Wright, J. 1980. "Anabolic steroids and athletics." *Exercise and Sports Science Reviews* 8:149–202.

About the Authors

SCOTT ROBERTS

Scott Roberts received his B.A. in physical education from California State University, Chico, his M.S. in exercise physiology from California State University, Sacramento, and his Ph.D. in exercise physiology from the University of New Mexico. He is a Certified Strength and Conditioning Specialist through the National Strength and Conditioning Association and an Exercise Program Director through the American College of Sports Medicine.

He is a leading youth fitness expert and the president of Scott Roberts Enterprises, Ltd., a fitness and education consulting company. He has been honored with numerous recognitions, the latest being a listing in the 1994–95 edition of *Who's Who in American Education*. He is a frequent presenter at national sports medicine and fitness conferences. He has published dozens of research papers, chapters in books, and articles. He is also the author of several books including *Developing Strength in Children: A Comprehensive Approach*, published by the National Association of Sport and Physical Education; *Clinical Exercise Testing and Prescription*, published by CRC Press; and *The Business of Personal Training*, published by Human Kinetics Publishers. He is also the coauthor of two successful college textbooks, *Fundamental Principles of Exercise Physiology: For Health, Fitness & Performance* and *An Introduction to Fitness and Wellness*, published by Mosby.

BEN WEIDER

Ben Weider was born in Montreal, Quebec, where he currently resides. Mr. Weider is recognized as one of the world's foremost authorities on strength training and bodybuilding. In 1945, Ben and his brother Joe Weider started Weider Sports Equipment and Weider Health and Fitness, which manufacture and sell their products throughout the world. The Weider organization has become one of the most recognized and highly respected names in the fitness industry.

Of all of Ben Weider's numerous accomplishments, the one most important to him has been the founding of the International Federation of Bodybuilders (IFBB). He remains the elected president of the IFBB, which has affiliates in 156 countries. Over his forty-eight years in the fitness and sports field, Ben Weider has become an international authority whose philosophy, books, courses, nutritional findings, and reports on athletic performance and general fitness have been recognized around the world.

He has made a major contribution to international sport, both through his research and his generous contributions to and support of fitness programs in numerous countries. He has donated complete training gyms to encourage young people and to assist institutions involved in sports research and training.

Index